three-toed gull

three-toed gull

Selected Poems

Jesper Svenbro

Translated from the Swedish by John Matthias and Lars-Håkan Svensson

Northwestern University Press
Evanston, Illinois

Hydra Books
Northwestern University Press
Evanston, Illinois 60208-4210

Printed in the United States of America
10 9 8 7 6 5 4 3 2 1

ISBN 0-8101-1895-5 (cloth)
ISBN 0-8101-2042-9 (paper)

LIBRARY OF CONGRESS CATALOGING-IN-PUBLICATION DATA
Svenbro, Jesper, 1944–
    [Poems. English. Selections]
    Three-toed gull : selected poems / Jesper Svenbro ;
translated from the Swedish by John Matthias and
Lars-Håkan Svensson.
        p. cm.
    "Hydra Books."
    ISBN 0-8101-1895-5 (alk. paper) — ISBN 0-8101-2042-9
(pbk. : alk. paper)
    1. Svenbro, Jesper, 1944– —Translations into English.
I. Matthias, John, 1941– II. Svensson, Lars-Håkan,
1944– III. Title.
PT9876.29.V348 A27 2003
839.71'74—dc21
                                        2003002232

The paper used in this publication meets the minimum
requirements of the American National Standard for
Information Sciences—Permanence of Paper for Printed
Library Materials, ANSI Z39.48-1992.

CONTENTS

ACKNOWLEDGMENTS

Acknowledgments are due to the editors of the following:

Kenyon Review ("Stalin as Wolf")

Parnassus ("Intimism" and "Hermes *Boukólos*")

Pleiades ("The Phonetics of Resistance" and "Classic Experiment")

Boston Review ("Rainbows" and "Saint-Marie")

Chicago Review ("Lepidopterology" and "The Socratic Problem")

Samizdat ("The Lake School Manifesto," "*La Mer,*" and "Idiolect")

Modern Poetry in Translation ("Three-Toed Gull," "The Sunlight on the Sound," "The Idea of the Sound," "Sound-Image," and "Stalin as Wolf")

Verse ("A Critique of Pure Representation," "Out There," "Ionian," "Idiolect," "*Poikilóthronos* Sappho," "The Pedestal," "The Lake School Manifesto," and "Mont Blanc")

boundary 2 ("Kit for an Orpheus Poem," "Syntagma," "Propertius Mistranslated," and "The Cotranslator's Dilemma")

three-toed gull

I

A CRITIQUE OF PURE REPRESENTATION

In order to restore to the words their semantic roughness
I told myself that there was no difference
between the stone I held in my hand and the word "stone"
clattering in language: I love the roughness of language
which marks its own presence and I claim passionately
that love of language in this sense
means resistance to pure repression.
Language is not a transcendental parameter, not god,
not a position from which the world "down there" can be gauged—
no, language exists within the world, opaque like a mountain,
and that is why I insist on the kinship of the stone
with the hard and obstinate word "stone." At some point
its presence must be acknowledged, its unevennesses be touched!
To each and every one the possibility of speaking on his own behalf
without being represented by somebody else
and to the words the possibility of representing themselves,
before their validity is extended to comprise the things
that together (and therefore together with the words)
constitute what we mean by the "world": deprived of its privilege,
language will attain weight. The stones are rumbling in the mountain.

MATERIAL FOR A GEOLOGICAL THEORY OF LANGUAGE

The vocabulary of the boulder ridges gives us an idea
of the history of the Swedish language during the ice age,
its *incubation period:* for a long time the words lay like stones
interspersed in the land ice, which melted and chafed,
receded, advanced, pushed the masses of words before itself
and like an enormous rock-shaping giant laid down
the principles of the language, the auxiliary lines of the rune carvers,
while in its interior it passed into fluent Swedish:
rivers of ice gushed in frigid tunnels,
dragging along linguistic material from different epochs,
proverbs like erratic blocks, grains of sand like punctuation marks,
and between them parts of speech, parts of stone, ground
against the harder rock of torrent's bed, against original language,
before they finally sank to the bottom and were stratified
under the surface of the Baltic ice lake.—Sun in the water line:
deep down the rivers of the land ice expelled themselves, depositing
their moraine of meanings, clay for conjunctions,
simplifying accidence and finally giving the nouns
a mobility they never knew in the primary rocks:
now they could roll, rotate, splash, and rumble,
before they settled in their places. (Language is disintegration,
but concurrent with disintegration there is construction
whereby crumbling material is given another meaning.)
The land slowly ascended. The reindeer trotted toward the north.
The first hunters who followed in their tracks
imitated the sounds of the melting water in their speech: for the first time
they uttered the words of the Swedish language
as they whirled around like the stones in a rapid,
clattering, rattling, knocking, clicking against teeth and palate
while the water spurted over stones and teeth,
through the echoing cave of the palate, full of stones and earth,
snorting through nostrils, rippling through throats.

THE PHONETICS OF RESISTANCE

In the history of the human voice the tendons of the skeleton
form the sinews, the abutments of different vowel systems
articulated around a constantly variable
yet incorruptible consonant; the skeleton itself
which with its vertebrae and bones, knuckles and knees
remains in its muteness, phonetically determinable,
when every vowel sound is gone.—Today I feel
the skeleton as a fundamental linguistic principle,
consonantal and articulate, with adjustable parts,
vibrating like a tuning fork when I cry in the wind,
humming in nose wings, collarbones, shinbones,
in thorax and shoulder blades, in skull and pelvis,
which are all held together by muscles and ligaments
to a steadfast presence in the soft language of the body!
The firmness of the backbone is the beginning of speech,
the voiced nasal makes the skeleton sound,
there is a phonetics that reveals the bond
between mountain and skeleton, rock and voice:
O reproducible paradigm which man after man
faithfully repeats like a code for all resistance!

STALIN AS WOLF

The position of the wolf was once secure in political theory
before it was driven by urbanization back to that final wilderness,
e.g., Siberia, where it lingers still without, to anyone's notice,
affecting contemporary politics. The plains sparkle in sunlight
as a helicopter rushes over the landscape: stunted birches
appear and disappear out on the snow-covered tundra
where all at once a wolf can be seen: it runs, it trips,
looks backward: someone has edited-in the hot gasps
of a dog to make us hear its fear: it is filmed close-up
and the camera is slightly jarred when the helicopter gunner
fires. The wolf is hit, rolls over in a swirl of snow,
then everything is still. Every year in the Soviet Union
more than twenty-two thousand wolves were killed, according to recent
statistics, and perhaps it is even yet a silent requirement
of Russian polity—menacing, inaccessible—which would explain
the cynical, obsessive precision of the hunting methods
both in the filmed sequence noted above, which,
with no comment, introduced a documentary on modern Siberia,
and also on the inner tundra where the wolf howls with hunger
in a nightmare only partially reclaimable. The facts about wolves
in Sweden at my disposal allow no conclusions, and yet,
within its territory, the wolf has developed local, independent
clans that have been identified as distinctive species. About
the role of the wolf in Russian politics from 1875 to 1953, however,
we know more than we suppose: Stalin's most wolflike characteristic
was distrust, which grew in proportions never foreseen by classical
lupine theory. As early as in Aesop we can find sufficient examples
to maintain that Stalin's role in political theory is basic:
the Wolf as Butcher, masters to perfection the partition technique
that is the base of political equality. The jaws of the Wolf
equal the Knife, and classical myth provides again the scenario
that ought to have haunted us earlier: hunting the wolf became
in the thirties a dominant trait in Soviet politics; he who wrote

"All power to the Soviets" three years before Kronstadt was now
the uncontested Butcher, the principle of absolute mistrust
had triumphed over Equality and the pack closed ranks around Stalin
in the whirling snowstorm. The Bolsheviks had certainly planned
an equitous banquet of wolves, but had forgotten the moment when Knife
turns into Weapon and the feast into its opposite. The gasps
haunt me, the plains sparkle, the film invades the memory:
am I willing to test that project now when Stalin's crimes
are rostered and surveyed, now when his bloodthirst, along with
the prospects that made it possible, have all been analyzed?
Zoologists can emend, on essential points, classical mythology,
refract the Stalinoid language: lacking both project and theory
the pack makes real the apothegm: "To each according to his need,
from each according to his ability." It refutes the picture
that pursues me and, in the end, obliges me to abandon
my language: gazing at Stalin, letting the wolf run off.

Translated by John Matthias and Göran Printz-Påhlson

LEPIDOPTEROLOGY

For a long time the butterfly held a prominent place in psychology
because of its caterpillar phase, its difficult sloughing,
and especially because of its pupa stage
which is a period of total paralysis of the will:
fascinated, people studied the frustrated dreams of the caterpillar,
such high-soaring dreams which corresponded so badly
to its ungainly earthbound body; observed
how the seemingly insoluble conflict between dream and reality
ended at last in total resignation
as the creature stopped eating, spun a shroud around its body,
and prepared to die. But in the deepest winter,
in the dried-out condition which is also that of taxonomy
when the pupa might have been classified
and placed in a showcase in some windless museum,
something unexpected, something totally unforeseen occurred
which gives us the right to believe in the impossible.
Georg Stiernhielm brandished his pencil, wrote "The Silk-Worm,"
and thus became the founder of lepidopterology on Swedish soil.
But in his poem psychology took a great step forward,
left the pupa stage, and established itself as a full-fledged science:
psykhē really means "butterfly," as you told me,
and warily it crept from its cocoon, its prehistory,
spread its wings and committed itself without fear to the wind.
So the poem is only the shroud left on the ground
where its miserable crumpled heap is only a measure
of victory announced by the butterfly's wings
now ablaze in the sun when it finally flies out of language
affirming its brilliant and dizzying love.

POLYPHONY

Among the available metaphors for the human body
the organ is the most renowned because of its sonority,
its several semantic registers and its construction
which imitates the human body down to the last detail,
from the high headwork with its powerfully resonant pipes
to the breastwork and choir, lip register and tongues,
while the organ-blower heart labors with enthusiasm
behind forward pipe works and the organ loft shakes—
manual shifts, runs, pedals at their humming rest
as notes get oxygen and yet more stops are pulled:
the *flauto dolce* of devotion draws its vertiginous line,
its ever bolder contrapuntal line which restores
to worn-out voices both the color and the timbre of the vocal,
meanings merge and separate, go silent and return,
are varied and repeated in semantics' altogether vast chorale:
the body is the organ that proclaims, singing, the bond
between polyphony and desire, mechanics and physiology—
vibrates and trembles in the bone pipes, organ pipes: I imagine
a polyphonic language as one single and enormous chord
in which all meanings have combined and love alone
inscribes its always freer line rejoicing over all the registers,
and summarizes the jubilant fact of your existence: the stops
are all pulled out, the body is transformed to ear and organ,
the organ into chest and throat, vocal chord and vowel,
while the heart blows and fills the organ's lungs with air,
the room resounds and creaks, whines and rumbles, blares and gleams,
the crescendo swell is opened wide, the chest heaves,
the plenitude of voices' overtones is infinite as humming,
shining rough and soft and buzzing weeping sound
achieves a polysemy of the body and your dear loved voice
is still perceived as the cantus firmus of existence
in anticipation of the echo when the edifice
of notes will be completed and the line run out into infinity.

FABLE

The draining of marshes and swamps has had a fatal effect
on the occurrence of frogs and storks, which has meant
a low-water mark for the ecologically sensitive fable.
Instead, other, truly energy-consuming genres
have taken their place as the typical expression of our time—
which, in a frog's perspective, is a result of the draining:
fast-growing pines have been planted in the frog's domain
and the resultant increase in the production of paper pulp
has favored, from a market point of view, more realistic fiction;
the writer who is therefore nicely high and dry
nowadays tactfully avoids any contact with the frog.
The ideal literary work of the forest is, under any circumstances
considering its, from the point of view of the words, woody stuff,
unfit as a locale for the lyrically shimmering frog
and is consequently never mentioned in recent literature.
Hence, the instances of the species that have survived
despite the draining are well disposed to a literary deluge
which might fill all distribution channels with water
and allow the frog—in the midst of a superficially shallow reflection—
to dive straight into the depth of language with a splash!
But above all the fable ought to give criticism a new flight:
the stork, which disappeared from Sweden sometime in the fifties,
must be welcomed back with its refined instrument
with which it has punctured a great many inflated individuals;
if in addition to this it is best left unsaid whether or not, in accordance
with widespread opinion, it might contribute to raising the birthrate,
the children will nonetheless benefit from the Fable.

COASTAL DEFENSE

The incident of the Soviet submarine in Goose Bay
raises the issue of how we want our archipelago poetry to look:
older metaphorical defenses from the fifties
may of course still have a function to fill
but a modern lyric coastal defense obviously must work
on entirely new premises, at once more efficient and discreet.
For a long time we were convinced that the enemy side
in case of an attack against the text would turn out to be too dense
to remain in its vast, seldom visited depth;
but with its classified sense, accessible only to a minority,
allegory has been superseded by a general polysemy
that permits maximal tactical mobility and makes it impossible
for the enemy to torpedo the lyrical basic sense in the usual way.
Given this way of looking at things, our linguistic sovereignty
becomes dependent on a reallocation of resources of our total defense:
Swedish literature's long-standing prioritizing of the air force
has gradually resulted in a visually advanced poetry
that has done well at international air displays,
but acoustic poetry has found itself in a backwater
forcing the navy to require subsidies for antisubmarine poems.
This is all the more reasonable as our realistic literature
as a result of its wish to "faithfully" map all of Sweden
constitutes a veritable security risk for our archipelago:
in report after report it has pirated information
that for a considerable period of time has put the motif out of action.
The nonaligned poetry cannot accept such an attitude
but scatters its meaning along coastal regions of such magnitude
that an enemy visitor sooner or later will run aground:
thus nature pays back in an unexpected way
the reverence that Swedish poetry has shown it for centuries,
and if the disabled vessel is heard to discharge long volleys of expletives
they only make columns of water rise between the islets—
until the bay once more lies perfectly blank as in the morning.

Against this extremely picturesque background it stands to reason
that we must increase our sensitivity to enemy movements—
on the pattern of foreign models we might for example introduce
the game of "sink-a-ship" as an obligatory item
but obviously measures of an entirely different kind will be necessary
if we want to train our hearing in a more literal sense:
therefore, the literary naval command has recently
followed the increasingly popular poetry readings with interest
and though the air staff has haughtily refused to listen
we have here a unique chance to prove our lyrical reliability
within the thirty-kilometer boundary once and for all.

INTIMISM

The export of ladies' underwear in France
has recently exhibited an unprecedented development
because of a bold investment in the mass production of garments
characterized by a past era's taste for details
and shown in classically black silk.
A similar development has not, alas, been experienced
in another traditionally strong export article,
namely poetry, and the explanation for this is no doubt
that the reserve of talent has permitted itself to be enchanted
by the intimist *écriture* that realizes its dreams
right on the female body through embroideries and lace.
Perhaps the poets should draw some conclusions from this
and, following an important idea in Mallarmé,
let their gaze reel at the nakedness of the page
which has not yet been dressed in typographical attire:
here anyone willing to make an inventory of the store
of typographical rosettes and leaf ornaments
with which printers ever since the sixteenth century
have been able to frame the undisguised flesh of the page
will find at his disposal a variety of stylistic tricks.
However, the flowery language must remain marginal
and strophic poetry take an absolute precedence
since it regularly uncovers undermeanings
precisely when the poet is most sparing of material,
that thin, very alluring black textile
under which the reader's fingertips now feel the presence
of the white body that is the object of reading,
literally grasped as an act of undressing.

HOMAGE TO T. S. ELIOT

At the outbreak of World War I Great Britain like a number
of other Western countries abandons the gold standard
which marks the beginning of the crisis in values
that "The Waste Land" documents with remarkable insight.
In the sudden absence of a general yardstick of values
Eliot the bank official turns to literature
where he finds the gold standard is still intact:
if language can preserve faith in its circulating signs
it is because of the considerable gold reserves of tradition
that permit us to redeem every word
at the value which the great poets have accumulated.
Not surprisingly, gold Latin poetry becomes the center
of his attention as he takes an inventory of history's sonorousness
which slowly but steadily is changed as to sense and volume
at the same pace as the gold production of our own era.
Although the gold standard nowadays is best seen as a utopia,
his own view of the relationship between tradition
and the gold deposits of the individual is still prevalent:
as we examine market averages on the stock exchange
where the rate of poetry is forever fluctuating
we feel a need for his long-range perspective
if we want to avoid misinvesting our talent.
For the speculator buys entirely pointless shares
in order to create a demand by artificial means
and is then able to dispose of them for a profit
after they have reached entirely inflated levels
thanks to the noise of the shouted quotes at the stock exchange.
This is indeed a perspective on our literature
that should lead to a slump and then a crash
resulting in a reconstruction of the national poetry market—
as if the gold standard were our brilliant corrective
to the despotism of fictive values!

HERMES *BOUKÓLOS*

In the hope that our project of reinterpreting the Hymn to Hermes
might find favor with one of our nine lyric ombudsmen
we here start on a tentative basis the transferal of cattle
which is the sign of really border-crossing poetry—
an experiment that we have had to postpone for a long time
as our metaphorical audacity has not by a long shot
permitted a cattle theft of this magnitude.
Now, however, the cattle herds of the Sun God
—a full-grown capital whose lowing is widely heard—
have suddenly proliferated at a rate expected by no one
which is why we too take up the shepherd's crook and openly explain
how we secretly have looked upon bucolic poetry,
for centuries capable of calving many-splendored interpretations:
all poetry is bucolic and the interpreter a cattle thief
who before restoring the cows he has stolen
makes them calve in secret and keeps the calves for himself!
True, Apollo sends the herds of poetry to graze
but the one-sidedly acoustic interest he takes in big cattle
which carefully fenced feed on the hills
confuses him when asked about the renewal of metaphor,
fundamental to the poetic subversion of our time;
on this point his half brother is perfectly up-to-date
ever since he stealthily signed the Surrealist Manifesto
one night at the beginning of the twenties:
what is Breton's "spark" if not the soundless sign
that Hermes with his wand has established a connection
between the two seemingly irreconcilable elements of the image?
Never is the poem's shower of sparks so wonderful as at night!
Not surprisingly, Hermes chooses the darkest hours of all
to resolutely seize the alphabet by the horns and push it
backward out of the fold of the old poems:
twenty-four cows with as many types of hooves
set off quickly in the pitch-dark of interpretation

where just as in the original text it is of paramount importance
that the Thief have more than one string to his lyre;
a few hours earlier, he invented the instrument
that determines the standard range of our own lyrical poetry
and rarely limits it to its highest register, suitable
for example to depicting the atmosphere among the gods
where they live, in Winckelmann fashion, at an altitude of three thousand
    meters.
Fortunately, the Cloud Gatherer discovered a little chap
who will forever break the monotony on Mount Olympus:
way down there on Earth he is seen leading his cattle
into a darkness that slowly begins to blink with fireflies,
punctuation marks in a childhood poem full of strange meetings
and so quiet that laughter can be heard at a distance of several miles:
is it Zeus chuckling at the prank of his newborn son?
For a moment, the ancient world holds its breath.
Only the tripping of ninety-six little industrious hooves
reveals to sensitive ears that border-crossing Hermes is on his way
and that the alphabetic order of tradition is now being rearranged
in a manner that makes constant use of chance.
Can tradition nevertheless transfer its meaning?
The hooves of our cattle are the same as those of antiquity
lining up their imprints in a lyrical verse of record length
from Mount Olympus in the north to Arcadia in the south,
where our Cowboy has stolen across the border, unseen:
things must work out as best they can! And in fact they do work out.
With its entire weight the poem narrates its cattle theft
and at dawn consists of the tracks it has left
on the path where now an irate Reader suddenly
is close on our heels in order to take possession of his herd—
right beside the precipice where all the poems still stand
and like thirsty livestock finally call for sound!

II

KIT FOR AN ORPHEUS POEM

In Sweden the words "lyre" and "sound" have been terms
that have given poetry its content during the sighing pine forest years
while it was busy licking its wounds in the wilderness:
faithful to a poetics of the lumber-language poem,
Orpheus is therefore an Oldforest pine on a clear-cut field,
aching and rent, but still standing upright at dawn
where furious tractors and chainsaws have razed everything else to the
    ground.
The fog is thick. There's a deadly silence among the stumps.
He might well be a seed pine, surviving lucky and green,
after having escaped one terrible forest fire after another,
an immense loner inhabited by birds and mice,
appealing to the Apollo who heals both lyre and sound:
Apollo *Terebintheús,* turpentine god, pine forest god,
allow him to play the woods out of the Underworld!
The Argonauts have long since fallen and been floated
down ink-blue rivers, toward the Botn or the Pontus—
once upon a time they rowed their *Schippe on creaking logges,*
the mast made of fir, its sail a starry sky,
and the woods resounded with their well-made songs,
ancient heroes walking toward the white beach of the Baltic.
There's a deadly silence on the clear-cut field. Brutal, isolated,
Orpheus has already turned his twig eyes inward—
when the sun suddenly creates a clearing through the fog
and the sundown slits of his eyes are full of resin:
once more Orpheus glances out across the woodland,
lets the morning dew glitter in his *Lay about the Sunne,*
Oldforest Orpheus with his lyre and overgrazed sound,
wild, terrifying, but finally healed and healthy
standing forever overgrown with torn lichen
and his head flown through by crested tit and buzzard,
by willow tit, crossbill, by owl and hawk
while the chars spawn in the brook at his feet.

CLASSIC EXPERIMENT

Seeing that so-called nature poetry ever since Romanticism
is best defined as a thoroughly realized simile
whose epic context simply has gotten lost,
we repeat on this winter day the experiment
of taking our stand in a simile near the middle of the *Iliad*
where the snowflakes are falling thick: the wind has calmed down,
the landscape with its ridges and woods, fences and fields
appears behind curtains of falling snow
and the acoustics of the image becomes just so hushed, intimate
that every connection with the exterior world seems broken.
The context that the image would have invested with life is gone,
the only thing left being the snowfall that won't cease:
this morning we heard that it would get more intense toward evening.
Soon the roads leading into the simile will be totally blocked!
Our isolation in the image seems in other words to increase
while at the same time the image itself begins to do likewise;
it is becoming capacious, inhabitable, the landscape has gained in depth:
no one can remember anymore its function in the poem
which once so presumptuously laid claims to the world.
The simile has become sufficient to itself, autonomous,
it seems capable of developing its own scenario:
for the shepherds have staffs, they even have bludgeons,
which will stand them in good stead when our critics arrive,
easy to club, lost as they are in the snowstorm.
Here it will come to literal blows! Far too long
the shepherds have accepted their subordinated place.
Who would have us believe that this is not the exterior world?
We are standing silent and thoughtful right in the middle of the text
of which the word "kingfisher" might already have formed part:
there is open water, an estuary, nearby
and the bird flies resplendently blue through the snowfall—
like a shuttle in the airy warp of the winter day!

MONT BLANC

For a long time linguistic obstacles hindered ascent of Mont Blanc
since the mountain, resting as it did "in snow-white majesty,"
seemed to demand humble subservience from those mountaineers
who in the eighteenth century tried to scale its peak—
until at last on one August night in 1786 *le docteur* Paccard,
accompanied by a guide and carrying in his knapsack a barometer,
managed to place his footwear at a height
of 4,807 meters. Thus the etiquette that had so far
prescribed relations with all manner of Highness was invalidated:
the Bastilles of cloud formations had already been stormed
and an immense, glowing stillness extended itself
for the most part over the Alps. Four years later
a young English wanderer walks past in the valley below
and for the first time sees the mountain in a moment
when the cloud cover splits and he has an unimpeded view:
while centuries of meltwater roar on and on
he measures, undaunted, its "singular height."
The last daylight lingers on its peak.
He resembles in this hour one who has reached his destination:
no second thoughts will revise the dizzying
small-print line of footmarks up to the peak
where Michel Paccard once and for all saw the evening sun go down.
Is it not here that a new language without syntax
with "glaciers," "waterfalls," "boulders," and "firs"
rises out of the dusky blue of existence?
He, Paccard, is standing lost in thought—
before the cold puts a sudden end to his meditations
and signals that he must descend along the little path
that nineteenth-century tourists will be so eager to tread.
Far down, folds and sheds, the turfed huts
of shepherds and hunters are waiting for him.
No eagle is yet to be seen against the radiant sky.

CYNEGETICS

Although we clearly didn't need a hunter's license to read Greek,
we were required anyway to spend a lot of time and energy
conjugating the verb *thēreúō,* "I hunt," in all the tenses—
until eventually in fact the landscape echoed with barking
and our entire band came walking through the dale
on a cold autumn morning when the sun was still low
and made the foliage of the trees shine high above us:
when that big liar, Autolycus, had chosen to stay at home,
we, his spear-bearing sons, briskly moved
to cross the present-tense system through all its active forms
and erected our hunting net to determine if a noun
duly inflected in the accusative might stick
in the meshes like prey. This morning
typified the freshness of a hundred October mornings,
the light over all the oaks and maples of Parnassus
was golden and archaic, and we moved with a freedom
that later we would never again experience: how our steps
echoed as we walked through the dale!
With the air itself transparent like shimmering water,
full of expectations we arrived at the aorist,
a "boundless" tense, we had been told;
here time was suddenly suspended. Up to now
we had only hunted with hesitation, unsuccessfully,
while the aorist designated a completed action—
in the past, the present, and the future.
Branches were broken, big piles of leaves were rustling,
from now on we would be successful in "hunting," our tracking sense
surpassing even that of dogs as we localized
the Wild Boar behind an unusually dense thicket
right out at the end of the text. There it was!
For years it had been ravaging the vineyards of the declinations,
terraced on the slopes of our hill,
rooting and grunting, attacking roots and trunks,

turning the garden patches of accidence upside down.
Now we were facing the beast in the dark:
it was heavy and menacing, bristled up in a rage,
and for a moment it was heard to grind its tusks,
visible as it made its spring and started off with a crash—
"we were being hunted" here in the passive, fled
and surely would have been goners had not Ulysses,
age fourteen, taken his stand in the path
and stabbed the boar with his spear in the aorist indicative.
Later we learned that it had bitten him on the thigh
so deeply that it left a clearly visible scar.
For the moment we were content to have escaped alive;
those who were really Swedish among us were of course most grateful
not to have had to hold the hunting spear—
which allowed them to clutch the Pointer with an iron grip.

—FOR PER SVENSON

THE VUOLLE OF MOUNT AMMAR

The spring sun sets conventions of the mountains rocking,
ice no longer holds, and the very Ammarfjället
—which in majestic isolation, in *pluralis maiestatis,*
has studied keeping silent all through winter—
is suddenly swept away by the singular form of the stream:
in every creek and rivulet the mountain proclaims "I" about itself!
So many rippling points of view on just one mountain,
so many sovereign rills that suddenly turn to waterfalls!
The melted snow overflows into a spring flood of emotions,
totally subjective and with no regard at all
for the *other person* of the riverbank
wet to the very skin as soon as the chanting begins!
For the spring flood is a yoik, the greatest of chants,
humming in rills and trickling in the sun,
merrily gurgling in the old and long-forgotten thickets,
gasping in the bog, crashing in snowdrifts,
roaring in all rapids, sighing in all stretches of smooth water!
Impossible to surpass in pitiless self-exposure,
it reveals the innermost secrets of the mountain:
one day it will be the inland ice near Rerrogaise that melts—
I am running, I am purling, I am shimmering, I am alive!
It turns to botany in its attempt to proclaim its love,
prepares a flowering as far up as the edge of ice
where the glacier crowfoot soon becomes the outer sign
of warm feelings even ice can have.
But the mountain knows the way to deepen its awareness of self,
how to make the melted snow expand, enriched by connotations,
and flow into the mountain lakes where ice has melted,
crossed by fish even in its coldest depths.
And one spring evening the flooding finally stops:
we are above the tree line, snow has disappeared, and the ground is dry.
A solitary reindeer bull stands scenting in the blue.

SWEDEN'S HELICON

The word in Greek for Vindelfjäll was *Helicon*
and the meadow under Big Mount Aigert close to Rödingvik
billowing with globeflowers seemed to prove the point:
this indeed was Sweden's Helicon and there we went
some thirty years ago for the express purpose
of learning how to yoik. And quite right too:
one summer night nine Clouds solemnly rolled down
the mountain slope and spoke to us and said: "Farmhand Laps
in the wilderness, we know the spruce woods' minor keys
and these will stand you in good stead in winter;
but if we wanted to, we might sing too the birch wood's major key."
And they handed me a birch wand and ordered me
to test the birch piano up on the Solåive
and to yoik in the present, the imperfect, and the future
about how Orpheus, the greatest of naoids,
one day came walking over the mountain,
invented the rainbow, and made its seven tones
sound across the Vindelåforsen, establishing
the highest level of the fir, the level
where the major chords of pure forest spruce begin—
white major chords, hard major chords,
piano chords under the cold sky.
White is the color of birch bark, white are the high summer clouds,
white as well are the whooper swans accompanying the Naoid
to the land of the mountains with its daylight nights,
helping him to find his Wild voice again
far away in the west, in the direction of Norway,
strolling in the interminable solitude.
One of the yoiks was to deal with him,
about how he lets his thoughts glide like the shade of a cloud
on a summer's day over the spruce forest, over the blue water of Tjulträsk
and the wide pastures of the reindeer above.

CAMPUS ELYSII

I was standing on Oulavuolie near the glacier crack
which is one of the many descents
into the Underworld, and I moved in my mind
—and therefore also in reality—to the other side,
as Orpheus had prescribed, before he dipped his frock in Lake Tjulträsk
and moved on west, toward the mountains "far away,"
covered with snow beneath the summer clouds, quite Elysian,
beyond the Flower Mountain and its ravine—
before the colors of the map run out, at the Frontier
where the black-and-white begins. This was the meeting place.
And there was a great silence.
For three days he was gone, accompanied by a bear
who had taught him how to leave his body while sleeping
and travel to the other side; for three days
the gnats stopped humming, the sun was dimmed,
the perianths of the flowers closed. The big grouse hunter
had now been transformed into St. Francis—
my father held his field flora, *Campus Elysii,* in his hand
and seemed to be calling out to me on the slope.
I had missed him my entire life.
And Orpheus lent me his frock, which had been dipped in Tjulträsk,
with its collar knitted the colors of the rainbow
(it is meant to protect you from the northern weather in death)
and I set off with my Bear.
There, above Skinnfällsträsk, I saw Nils Mattias Andersson
enveloped by the smoke near his arra, his gaze turned inward,
saw my grandmother who told me
that the lakes of the beyond were as blue as those of life,
saw the young Linnaeus marveling still
at the exuberance of the mountain world and its miniature herbs.
My field flora was scented with the flowers it contained
and the tall mountain was radiant. Until my father
showed me how, hanging in a winged seed,

I would glide back to my starting point:
when he landed there he was me. And when Orpheus then
put his tuning fork to the bedrock of Lapland
suddenly all the numberless gnats once more started to hum
and together they lifted Västerbotten an octave
—its forests, mountains, and bogs—
and held it there for the whole of the summer soaring.

POIKILÓTHRONOS SAPPHO

Sappho was to yoiking what Homer was to epic—
or so we were taught as late as the sixties
when we attended the school at Cape Dårra,
one "more central" than the other institutes
to the renewal of tradition: the grass was whispering,
somewhere purling of a brook was heard and seemed
to promise a freshness not to be found anywhere else.
Smoke rose from the cape, from our hearth of simple stones,
and one day Sappho actually appeared—
while I dozed, it was summer:
she was small and dark skinned, dressed in Lap gear,
which was so bright a blue it seemed unreal;
her collar and breast had been knit in colors of the rainbow
and I understood: this was *poikilóthronos* Sappho,
the "artfully attired," who here at the nomad school
was weaving poems of boughs and the fibers of roots,
solid stanzas of willow and birch, of silver thread,
with pewter embroideries and reindeer horns, with moon and stars—
such as you can see in early autumn nights
when the Milky Way finally appears.
Smiling, she explained that night was the letter *a*
and invited me to use the *a* in every yoik.
This was our pact. And the moon shone among glistering stars,
shone on the valley and over the forested heights.
On the other side of the lake the cows were sleeping in their byres.
How muted and distant our voices seemed!
And when the moon had set, a nightjar descended the slope
just over the treetops, among the stars
where its silhouette could for a moment be discerned.
And if you stretched your arm you might reach all the way up,
so near did the stars seem to be,
illuminating there our innermost dreams.

RAINBOWS

Once the memory of the Spring Flood had receded
I noticed that on account of "faulty navigation"
Noah's Ark had gotten stranded on the top of Big Mount Aigert:
despite its considerable dimensions no one seemed to notice it
stuck there as it was with its stern tipped slightly upward,
leaning over the precipice. All the mountain animals
had begun to pour out of its interior,
and seemed almost to tumble down the steeps—
lemming and lynx, bear, squirrel, fox,
otter, moose, and wolverine and certainly not least the hare
who in the early morning sun down on the Dårra headland
was to lift his prayer to the rainbow
there among the twinkling water drops of the grass.
Rimbaud himself came walking down the mountain
dressed in a blue coat common among Laps
who lived and fished in Norway say a century ago;
he was bareheaded and his lank black hair
blew like wild in the western wind!
When we shook hands, I felt at once that his were strong.
He was in high spirits despite the grounding
and he told us he'd been heading "northward," *Nor-wege*—
toward Norway in the etymological sense—
to study fjords, rains, and sun right on the spot.
His real name of course was Rainbow!
That's why Lake Tjulträsk suited him so perfectly;
everything was here, and most of all there was a slope
that he was planning to use one day in his paraphrase
of the Gospel according to Matthew, where
Jesus feeds the people
on the mountainside: five loaves and two fish
would suffice, no need for a miracle at all
since there were only such a few of us
here at the tree line, among the increasingly whiter
silver birches.

ILLUMINATION

I never caught a glimpse of the goddess' body,
only divined its immensity in the blue—
Aphrodite was like Tjulträsk where she was mirrored,
smiling imperceptibly among the whitest clouds
that floated far down there in the heavenly depth.
When I raised my eyes I could not see her face,
the light was too strong, and around her head
stood a halo of snow, of shining sun.
But her cloak was knitted with thousands of birds
which now late in May celebrated their wedding on the mountain—
where the heat of spring all at once had released
an incessant fluttering of little glistening wings,
the wings of small birds in the region of the tree limit:
everywhere you could hear the fanning of wings
and a careful whistling in birches and osiers.
She was this sudden wave of heat
that for a moment let everything merge with everything else,
that let the south be crossed with the north, the west with the east,
high be crossed with low, near with far.
Now Lapland longspurs, bluethroats, yellow wagtails,
willow warblers, meadow pipits, redstarts, wheatears were coupling;
they chittered chromatically among the flowers of mountain flora,
shining in yellow, white, and lilac—
on the azure cloak of the goddess, already lined with green.
The sun was warm, hardly ever wanted to set,
the nights were full of midsummer light;
in our dreams we were little birds, flowers, clouds,
and sometimes you could see a ripple on the water—
a very faint ripple on the glimmering water
indicating that two clouds high up there
were dreaming exactly the same dream
and that a wonderful gust of wind traversed it.

THE LAKE SCHOOL MANIFESTO

The Lake Tjulträsk school was based on a simple principle:
the Homeric simile was an "objective correlative"
that made us stay up late at night
and attentively watch the stars of the autumn sky—
we wanted to come closer to that passage in the *Iliad*
where the Trojans had lighted fires on the plain beneath the city,
confidently waiting for the arrival of dawn.
How distant those old heroes seemed!
But the reality of the simile was shockingly near:
Homer himself seemed to be standing there on the mountainside,
right in the moonlight, with the strong hands of a craftsman:
and in a low voice we began to plan with him
an entire anthology of pastoral similes
in which we would suppress the initial "like"—
these were Homer's *Lyrical Ballads,*
liberated at last from the pan-Hellenism
that had oppressed them. For intuition in the *Iliad* was lyrical:
the saga of the Trojan men was an immense, derailed poem on nature
that might very well have taken place here,
while the yellow leaves of the birches, the red leaves of the rowans
fell and fell like generations of heroes.
And one morning the peak of Big Mount Aigert shone completely white.
Rather than return to the woodlands in the east
we decided to stay right here near the tree line—
in the region of the white birch bark
where all the camps were abandoned at this time of year.
The epoch itself had been sacrificed. Yet the hare in his winter fur
would escape the eye of the soaring bird of prey
when the snow started falling on all the similes
and the local tradition once more coincided with the rush
of the Matsoljokk on the other side of the lake,
so silent underneath the clarity of one night's glaze of ice.

ONCE-ONLY MUSIC

From a long-ago September I recall the first performance
of what seemed to be a piece
of concrete music, the last movement of a suite in B-minor
for flute and orchestra, executed by a solo flute
and a bleating flock of sheep near Lillbjörkstugan
with its silver-gray southern wall as backdrop:
the composer's name was Johann Sebastian Jokk
and the listening sheep seemed to like
his music: the flute was made of silver
and as long as Lake Stora Tjulträsk down below,
the ensemble quality of the birches contributed in their way
to the soughing of the first performance. Their leaves were green,
green the meadow, and green still the late summer mountains
in this moment with the silver tone of the flute
and the deep blue surface of the lake farther down—
mirrored in miniature in the recently polished surface of the flute.
The listening sheep were now green, now blue—
perhaps that was why their wool
had the qualities of silver and could absorb
the colors of the strangely shining afternoon.
And the flautist on the hill sent his sequence of tones
"as easy as can be" to show the mountain world
that he had found the acoustics excellent,
made his spring among the fence poles of the musical systems,
filled his lungs, played, let his fingers
run at a sixteenth-note measure like eager tripping
up and down the paths of the notes, fixing
the mountain slope like a music rack, in wildly glowing sunlight,
while just behind the birches Apollo
tactfully took his place in stocking feet to listen
to this incomparably keyed once-only music—
which glided in a final whole note right across the lake.

HYPERION

When the Swedish bus poets discovered that Hyperion had gotten on
they wanted to eject him: which turned out to be unfeasible
as he had actually bought a ticket:
the driver was unbending on that point.
The bus poets therefore got off in protest
just before Ruskträsk, and so
our transport problem seemed to be disposed of.
However, we had underestimated the reaction of the Hyperion readers:
by way of rumor they knew that their hero
was aboard the bus and were now standing on the roadside
a stop or two before Sorsele:
and demanded that he too step off the bus,
this in their view too trivial
a means of transportation. As Hyperion was immune
to their "weighty reasons" they grew mightily enraged,
calling his very identity into question:
was it really *Hyperion* sitting
on the seat just behind the driver
hunting for something in the landscape—
a sun ray through the swamp's bank of mist,
a squirrel on a wonderfully swaying bough?
Now it was late morning. It was time to change buses
at the most trivial of stations.
O soundless days at Sorsele, waiting for the bus
among pines and silver birches, with only the clouds for company!
We rode along the Storvindeln. We passed Mount Hemfjäll,
where I once more felt the bedrock tottering beneath me.
Hyperion and I were the only passengers.
A little while later he got off,
swiftly put on his knapsack, and made for
the mountain through the birch wood,
his back as immense as the landscape.

THE FOUNTAIN OF DARK MOUNTAIN

For a long time I kept wondering how to write
the poem about Skotoessa, the poem about *The Fountain*
of Skotoessa, whose miracle waters
the ancients had told us about. Then one day I understood
that the name meant "Dark Mountain" and that the fountain
was found in the middle of Lapland. Its waters
really did possess the power to heal wounds;
and if you lowered even the deadest branch of wood
into its healing, cool, and silver darkness
then it started turning green once more. I came to this place
wholly unprepared, with my wound
and staff of birch one summer's day—
when the sun was warm on the back and the lakes shone blue:
then I didn't understand why the place
was called Dark Mountain. Maybe it was the name
of a forgotten site with no location on the map—
some mountain of the mind where I had to walk alone
without a guide along a path that led
through juniper bushes, dwarf birches, and osier.
But I did get to Dark Mountain;
and I saw the fountain there. And I touched the water
and felt its power; then I dipped my staff
into its silver shimmering depths;
and it was healed, birch leaves burst once more from its bark.
And my father, whom I hadn't seen in forty years,
was standing near me, I knew it without seeing him;
and urgently he asked me to remember
"him whose face is like the sun."
I was overcome by a terrible irresolution.
Dark Mountain was plunged in a deepening shade.
But when I turned around I stood there blind—
face to face with the Sun.

III

THREE-TOED GULL, SIGHTED NEAR
THE LIGHTHOUSE OF KULLEN

I was familiar with the sense of soaring from the music
of Lars-Erik Larsson: he must have seen
the same water surfaces as I, been filled by the same light
along the same curving coastline,
and felt the slowly rising movement of the summer
in an outer world that already was an inner one:
it was as if one stood and looked northwest
where the northern Sound has imperceptibly become the Kattegat
on a day when all the sea is placid and the sky light blue
and a hazy fog seals the horizon—
the blank shining groundswell
with a single floating tuft of seaweed
or a bit of plank that heaves
slowly mirroring itself, while the sea's
cool and intensely shining mist
rises up in microscopic crystals of salt—
soaring in the air where the Sound opens out
on an unfathomable beyond and a single three-toed gull
which, battered from some afterworld of flight,
comes in view as flying's sole survivor
gliding inland toward the lighthouse at Kullaberg—
Winddriventhing at rest in the bluest of hazes
or perhaps an optical illusion in the prisms of the lighthouse
open toward monotony of air—
all alone on a summer's day,
which sees the loss of the horizon,
takes a giddy gyroscopic turn, and topples over in memory
without a sense of anything but height and depth
as if shutting its eyes to the infinite
with wings spread wide, rising and sinking and soaring
seems to free itself at last
from the immense and sparkling blue.

SOUND-IMAGE

The irregularity of my piano playing sometimes means
that when I sit down in front of the keyboard
and begin to play a few bars of some piece
I may have played for years—a prelude, a minuet—
I suddenly lose my memory of it:
a great chasm of forgetfulness then opens up
and the music is silent. How is memory
to be restored? The sound-image seems to have disappeared.
One way of making the music return
has been to think of the room where I once learned
to play in my childhood: to concentrate—
not on the music but on the room
with its cool freshness on a summer's day
when the sounds of the neighborhood turn silent and the sunlight
from the room opening onto the garden is reflected, vibrates
there in the dimness of a deep green velvet,
is refracted in the chandelier's iridescent prisms, reflected
without tinkling on the ceiling or the walls.
Behind me are the pastel painting of sailboats on the Sound,
the sofa purchased at the turn of the century in Helsingborg,
mirrors and silver, and I feel as well my grandmother's presence
beside me on a chair near the keyboard
where my fingers now are running easily and without trembling
across the white keys and the black
as if I were walking on a well-known path,
a passage, corridor, or staircase just now rediscovered
in my memory's furthest recess, in its sounding labyrinth,
and she is seventeen as in that photograph,
her curly hair pinned up, the suggestion of a smile—
the year must be 1900, her lace collar is white
and she is looking at me with her large gray-blue eyes,
looking at me with love.

IONIAN

The light in the north Sound was "Ionian"—
greedily we repeated the word although we didn't know
what sense to make of it at all—
until one day we cycled seaward on our bikes
from well inland and at last high upon a hill beheld
the summer water resting there against the light,
glittering intangibly as far as we could see—
as if a massive door had opened on infinity.
Ionian was the tone throbbing in the sky,
Ionian the dialect of waves, Ionian as well
the dry white sands along the beach. We had found
the tone that seemed to hold reality together,
like a hub that sings around its axis
with a note of an "Ionian" frequency—
while Ionian white clouds scudded quickly on the wind
in formation spreading out across the sky.
On days like that you would see the pillars of Heracles
shimmering unreal in the distance like mirages
where the Sound is narrowest: the streams
were swift and deep up there, the water
cold and flowing from the depths
into the inland sea, into its warm and amber summer.
The clouds: an Ionian archipelago in the north.
It was as if our very thought had ionized—
the most trivial ideas now were charged electrically
and seemed to wander slowly, white to blue.
Everything was colored by the adjective and it was spoken
ever and forever over whining voids, increasingly monotonous,
so often used that finally it
became unusable. Invisible in white. As if the door
were closed and painted over, sealing
our Ionian epoch. And after many years I passed it
and was able without strain to lift it off—

I took down the lintel, the doorposts and threshold:
all that remained was the keyhole
now that the light of my late summer afternoon
had neither attributes nor hinges. No keys, no handle.
All the paint had flaked off and was gone.
The evening sea was wide and blue. Its warmth
a feeling over my entire face.

THE CLOUD

For a long time my notion of reality seemed
to be too meteorologically inclined
to lay any claims to depth:
it was as though it were too close
to all those noncommittal conversations about clouds
with which we often fill the sky.
But such was not the case. My affinity
with the clouds which in the later 1950s glided
wonderfully and slowly over the street I knew so well
—the facades, windows, echoes from the yards—
was fervent: to that extent I knew where I stood
far down in the shadowy depth of the street
in the summery town that had seemed
depopulated just a while before
although it was really always full
of those "who now are shadows and gone."
And instead of feeling regret for those who were dead
I suddenly felt a secret joy
where I stood surrounded by them
in the intensely shimmering darkness:
my happiness seemed comparable
to that of the cloud up there, slowly gliding
through the sky of a late summer afternoon
growing and growing in its sun-drenched whiteness
while I was left in the realm of shadows
and it was always August, late 1950s—
the cloud passes, sunlit and eternal
in its realm of light for which I have always longed,
and I understand that my longing is the cloud
that keeps on growing, growing
until, my eyes closed, I am filled with its light
and drift away—
although, shadowlike, I'm still down here
in the deep cleft of the street.

AUTUMN DAY AT HILDESBORG

Certain days we used to go up north toward the Glumslöv hills,
taking the way along the sea leading to the Brickworks
and the Valley, which seemed to provide
the very props we needed
for our bellowing rural poems. Sometimes
it was difficult of course to find the connection
between our experience and our language:
only "the whimpering of a pine tree" seemed for example
to correspond to our predicament in the wind
one autumn day when without a single metaphor
we came out of the woods on a path
at the very top of the eroded verge near Hildesborg.
And still the sea must have been foaming with metaphors
against the pebbles of the beach down there!
While we walked on the path the barbed-wire fence to the right
turned in our minds to a genre boundary
even though the cattle had left the pasture beyond for the fall.
Therefore without thinking twice we jumped right over it
and went up to the softly rounded crest of the hill—
when a huge black bull came charging
in our direction. As I reconstruct the events
one of us must have been wearing a scarf
which I persist in imagining was *red*.
A red scarf! That was enough to make
the bull pursue us at full speed over the fence,
enraged at the conventions
in which he had rashly been imprisoned.
We stood there on the verge for one terrifying moment
before we chose to tumble down. How the sand whirled about our ears!
Later we saw him standing there high above us,
snorting, with his head over the fence.
Was that my "red scarf" streaming from his horns?

OUT THERE

Ever since I started writing poems
(and probably even further back than that)
the words "out there" have seemed to carry distant messages:
as if a strange power emanates from them
when I say them over slowly deep inside
or write them down, lending equal emphasis
to both as two short words.
Over the years I have slowly understood
where this charge is coming from, from what landscape
they derive their supernatural light.
In memory I return to my native city,
Sturegatan 1, fourth floor, the window to the yard
with a view of a little pond in the north-northeast:
about three miles away you could just see Härslöv
nearly a hundred yards above the sea
while in the elongated heights to the east
the hills of Rönneberga rose
beyond my vision. This was the view
from the nursery I shared with my sisters,
from the world I knew so well
with its doll's house and my hobbyhorse
on green rockers . . . I saw out there
on many late afternoons in my childhood
the landscape bathing in sunlight.
And I imagined that two cyclists had stopped out there;
and if I could see them so clearly, it must mean
that they were supernatural in size
where they stood gazing in the direction of the Sound
which was beyond the range of vision too.
They are my parents who have just gotten off their bikes,
my father in a shirt with rolled-up sleeves:
looking at the glitter of the sea with screwed-up eyes,
my mother with closed eyes, in a summer dress:

the mild summer light falls on their faces,
so beautiful that in that moment
they must have been touched by the divine—
while the breeze fills my father's loose white shirt
and slowly blows through the locks
of my mother's hair, who is still closing her eyes
in the light of the late afternoon.

IDIOLECT

In my use of the word "world" there is a strangeness
that I have never been able to shake:
the word carries a hopefulness
that strictly has no foundation
in the real world.
The world being what it is!
For although I know it cannot be used
in the sense I want to give it
it is the same picture that faithfully
returns in my memory
whenever I pronounce it to myself—
it is the light space over my childhood,
white April sun over a province
whose horizon trembles in the distance:
the world rests over there.
It is the late 1940s. In those days
I went to Sunday school every week
in our northern Galilee. To me
Palestine was still a country
with heights, fields, and rivers such as ours;
and by a miracle
the hills of Rönneberga just outside of town
became the light-green mountain
where on one spring day Jesus
had said to his pupils: "Go out into the whole world!"
Languages were buzzing in the air.
Jews, Arabs, Cappadocians, Egyptians!
We were in the Holy Land,
coltsfoots were blooming
along the ditch banks of the world.
And among all the tongues that I heard
was also the sound of my own.

THE SUNLIGHT ON THE SOUND

Because my father had grown up in Helsingborg,
I had the strongest feeling every time we visited
of his belonging there:
his kinship with the city so impressed me
that I made it mine.
From my grandmother's apartment
we had an excellent view of the Sound:
Kronborg Castle was straight across
in the sun, its roofs green with verdigris.
Ships of different kinds steered to the north and south.
Ferries and sailing boats shone white . . .
This is what I am thinking of this morning
having woken from a dream
that seemed to take place on the beach
just north of Helsingborg.
My dream is like a poem of light.
And every time I go over it in memory
it remains unchanged:
not a boat can be seen at sea,
not a single person on the land.
The sea and sky are blue. A southwesterly breeze.
I am standing on the sandy beach in the sun
and seeing the horizon open in the northwest on immensity beyond.
I turn my gaze to the west
and I am saying aloud in my dream
where for an instant words and visual impressions
correspond in every way: *The Sunlight on the Sound.*
In my dream it is as though these words
composed a truthful
and exhaustive statement about the world—
as if I wouldn't be able to add the smallest adjective
without obscuring the sun.
I couldn't add a single word.
Nor could I subtract one.

THE IDEA OF THE SOUND

When, sometime in the early sixties,
we tried to reformulate the idea of the Sound,
Paul Eluard's poem "Bathing woman
from light to darkness" was our only axiom:
with just this poem for our intellectual baggage
we took the boat to Hven
one May morning in a western wind
with "Eluard clouds" sweeping across the entire sky—
in joint formation as far as you could see!
When we started it was early.
The day was a circle drawn with a pair of compasses.
We walked along the long beach of the island widdershins:
saw how the maritime light would change
for every hour in the periphery:
this was "the order of splendor, the order of the stones,"
mentioned in our poem.
And we could hear a drawing pencil being used—
or was it the sea that made this whispering sound?
Imperceptibly we went to meet the sun.
In our thoughts the idea of the Sound
—two beaches, streaming salt water—
appeared as a dazzling abstraction
of lines, angles, infinity.
We felt the salt on our skin, the sand in our eyes . . .
For a long time the sunlight cut its prisms.
But when, late in the afternoon,
we finally reached the point in the poem
that lies about a kilometer south of Bäckviken
the sun was sinking, the sandy cliffs
already casting long shadows toward the east
across the green depths where we had arrived in the morning.
The stone blocks that we were sitting on
were still warm from the sun,

all we heard was the roar of the sea,
the corrosive wind had exhausted all our senses . . .
Here the island was suddenly left to the waves:
no houses could be seen,
the bay before us seemed to have gone out—
and as in ancient times it would once more have been possible
to go to sleep in the sea.

COWPATH

Scania had many secret cowpaths,
meandering under foliage, humid, where you could
pass unseen with your lowland cattle.
Only the trotting hooves and breaking twigs
suggested that something might be afoot.
Like for example on a certain Monday evening in the fifties:
one of my cowpaths began "down in Tröllare,"
which is a place that for quite a number of people
for some considerable time has had a definite meaning.
But Tröllare is not shown on any map,
lying as it does with its oaks just south of the railroad track
between Göinge-Fridhem and Önnestad
in the northeast corner of Scania.
I found myself down there on a mission
to select a black-and-white heifer,
walk it all the way to Kivik
and, on arriving, sell it.—It is the end of July.
The nights are much darker now, but tonight
the full moon has appeared and is shining
across the whole of the vast landscape,
yet without revealing the lie
of my path. The first problem
to be solved is how to cross the highway
between Kristianstad and Hässleholm. That proves simple enough:
no traffic to speak of on this Monday night.
I am walking behind the cow with my hazel wand.
Our way leads due south up along the hills.
Somewhere in a glade up there
as I pause and turn around
I see the plain stretching out in its immensity:
it is like seeing it appear with all its details
through a midnight-blue filter on a summer's day!
Except that not one human being can be seen and

animals are sleeping standing up in moonlit pasture fields.
In leafy groves down there you can see farms . . .
In a henhouse there's a cackle and then again it is still.
And out there in the shade of the courtyard's
single drooping chestnut tree lies Bojan too,
the St. Bernard, asleep. I know her well:
perhaps it is she who is right now dreaming of me
and not me dreaming of her.
A bird shifts some twigs among the leaves of her tree.
At the village of Önnestad the dairy woman
has put out a bowl of moonlight for the hedgehog.
The hedgehog quickly empties it
and without looking up at the moon or the maid
—who is also dressed in white—turns around
and slouches away to its thicket.
The trees by the railroad station are dark in the moonlight.
And they have taken the roof off the school assembly hall:
the pianist plays the *Moonlight Sonata*
quite soundlessly, "leaving the audience spellbound"
as tomorrow's newspaper will say.
As for myself, I am right now on my way to Tollarp!
That it is at least ten kilometers away doesn't worry me;
that it is probably not possible
to walk all the way Tröllare–Kivik in a single night
accompanied by a heifer worries me
even less. I am out on a mission.
It is so silent that right now you can hear
how a leaf is turned in the great big book
up there. I have sat myself down on a garden bench.
Sitting next to me is Martin P. Nilsson,
whom I never met in real life.
His face is plunged in darkness.
The heifer is standing next to us, there is water to drink
in a cavity right beside us, smooth
with a trembling moon. Meadows and thickets

radiate darkness. The sound of a motorbike dies out far away.
He is telling me now that he repents
certain theoretical thoughts about race he expressed
in the twenties and thirties; it is not for those
he wants to be remembered.—Then he disappears.
The broadleaf trees are oddly still.
Once more you hear a leaf being turned
in the big dark book up there.
The passwords tonight are "fork" and "silence."
The heifer trots off; I jog-trot myself to catch up.
When I finally come up to the highway
I am quite near Ovesholm,
on a long and moonlit avenue where I think I can walk unseen
since no one is out at this time of night.
But there I am wrong: down at the crossroads
there are people moving around! I hear their laughter,
a car door slamming shut. Too late to steal away
with the cow . . . We have been discovered!
It is the nine Girls of the Linderöd ridge who are standing there;
somehow, though, there now are only three.
They are in high spirits as if they have come from a party.
The youngest is dressed in a summer frock
with little green and white squares; of course
I do not really see they are green
but I seem to have always known that they are.
I tell myself in a loud voice
that she is "a rattling attractive girl";
it must have been Apollo who put that phrase on my tongue
and I hope she didn't hear me.
Oh yes, she heard me all right; and yet she acts like she didn't.
Now they want to buy my cow. At what price?
They laugh and promise me "a rattling good price."
And then things happen fast: I sense the youngest one's
laughing summer body next to mine,
she is naked under her frock,

she must have warm moonlit thighs which I don't see
and yet seem to see quite clearly.
At that very moment I wake up! I must have fallen asleep . . .
I think of the darkness of soundless foliage
that offers complete shadow against the light of the moon.
And without moving, with eyes shut,
I seem for a moment to make the plot
of my dream cohere to the smallest detail . . .
The heifer, needless to say, is gone; she has dissolved in the dark,
in the great, nameless darkness
and may not even ever have existed.
How the moonlight glittered on our path!
But at the end of each cowpath there is a new poem—
and readable even in moonlight,
in moonlight that lets the shadows of the syllables vanish.
Here I am not very far from the beach,
illuminated and strangely deserted in the night.
Far out there the moon irradiates the sea
which amplifies its light a thousandfold:
when I approach the dunes from the woods up there
I suddenly feel it over the whole of my face—
while the swell of the Baltic
with a captivated whisper withdraws,
is sucked back, collects itself, flushes the beach once more,
silver-plating the smallest object on its way.

IV

INTERIOR WITH A VIOLIN

One day I shall return to Copenhagen to verify
the blues in Matisse: I must discover
if the three blue color planes in my reproduction
of his "Interior with Violin" are correct.
On many Saturdays in Copenhagen
I would lose myself in this picture at the National Museum.
It was like my window on an unreal Mediterranean.
The darkest blue was the case lid of the violin
which was placed on an armchair to the left of the room.
The blue of the bottom and edge of the case
was a shade lighter at least.
And the blue one saw from the window,
the blue of the surging sea, was the lightest blue.
A triad of blues! Now it so happened that my own violin case
in which my old violin now and then still lies
was exactly the same; and the instrument was such a reddish brown
that I confuse it with the violin of the picture.
As an aid to my memory I have a reproduction,
the color plate illustrating the entry "Matisse"
in a dictionary printed in 1952—
in which the year of the artist's death does not yet figure.
How the room shivers from light in my picture!
The summer out there is so gigantic
that it can only be guessed: you see
a beach with a palm and a stretch of sea through the window
—the left shutter is closed, the right one open—
and I understand that the living dusk of the room
must be synonymous with the interior of the violin
which sensitively intercepts some very distant sounds:
the children's voices on the beach, the sound of the waves
one particular day at the beginning of the century—
when my father is eight years old
and has just begun to play the violin. The instrument that is now mine.

The room is a camera obscura, vibrating
with indirect light: slats of the closed shutter
are shining poles in the dark. Yesterday I took out
my old violin case, opened it,
and placed my violin in the blue.
Suddenly it got dark; I seemed to stand in the midst of the picture
unable to utter a word.

SAINT-MERRI

Apollinaire's poem about the flute player
who, accompanied by "a bevy of languishing women,"
walks the streets around Saint-Merri one day in May 1913
caused problems for the translator:
some of them I thought I could master
simply by heeding
the topographical directions given in the poem itself
and walk the same way the flute player does
from the moment when he unexpectedly
turns into rue Aubry-le-Boucher from the "Sébasto"
—boulevard de Sébastopol—
until he disappears into a house
over on the rue de la Verrerie.
So, half a century after Apollinaire's musician
I turned into the street
carrying the Pléiade edition in my hand.
It was just before the block was leveled and rebuilt.
Today it is difficult to imagine what it was like:
ramshackle houses all propped up
by makeshift supporting beams,
the gutter full of refuse and garbage . . .
When I arrived in the rue Saint-Martin
what then was called the "plateau Beaubourg" opened up:
an enormous space full of parked cars
and heaps of trash as after a market day.
The sun was blazing down.
A gushing hydrant turned the street into a lake.
I traced the flute player's shimmering steps,
continuing north on the rue Saint-Martin
until I realized that I had come
to the vanished intersection at the rue Simon-le-Franc
where the flute player stopped to drink
from the fountain on the corner of the street.

But the rue Simon-le-Franc now passed directly
through the present Centre Beaubourg
and so this part of its extension
was no longer there.
My street corner was theoretical. Where was the fountain?
Just here, however, the flute player and I turned around
returning down the rue Saint-Martin
the same way we had come.
The flies led their fly lives
in the sunshine on the plateau Beaubourg.
If you came near them, you could see their dazzling splendor . . .
I passed before the portal of Saint-Merri,
a medieval church
with demons and angels.
Today no bells were heard from the tower
as the flute player turned to the left by the corner of the church—
into the longish rue de la Verrerie.
The women following him
moved to the sound of his flute, it says;
they had flocked together like mad from the little side streets
of which there are so many on this block
and had kept on gathering.
They had names like Ariane, Amine, and Pâquette
with the variant Paquerette—"Daisy," that is.
When I had turned the corner myself
I wanted to know where I was:
first I had a look in the Pléiade volume and then
at the street sign.
The opening of the rue de la Verrerie
seemed to grow larger like a stage: I remained standing
in the middle of the plot
without understanding what it was all about.
The summer afternoon had an acoustics all its own—
murmuring voices, breezes, the odd laugh.
A woman was improving her makeup.

With her back to the street
another one talked to somebody in the dark
at the side entrance of the church,
a third one slackened her pace, watched the youth
who had the Pléiade edition in his hand:
was he walking around here reading the Bible or what?
The daisy smiled as if requiring an answer
this sunny afternoon—
when it suddenly dawned on me what she was up to.
"*Tu viens?*" I was so surprised by her question
that I couldn't think of anything to say!
Luckily, I had the poem to think about
and continued straight ahead—
until I suddenly thought I had found the door
where the flute player had entered
accompanied by the women . . .
The house dates from the sixteenth century.
Here Apollinaire and the priest of Saint-Merri
had entered half a century before me.
Of course they found neither the flute player nor his women.
There was a remarkable stillness.
Now they had been gone for a long time,
and the yard was even more deserted than then:
the wagons of the haulage contractors had disappeared
and the windows had been nailed up.
Only I was here.—And so it will be for you
and for you and for you
who will once more take this walk
in the block around Saint-Merri.
But as yet you are standing in the echo there
of the flute's faintest note.

PONT MIRABEAU, CIRCA 1895

The lady on the Pont Mirabeau raising her arm
to salute us, waving in a painting by Henri Rousseau,
seemed to me unsurpassed in melancholy:
the afternoon sky a golden ground
beyond the bridge master's house to the left,
beyond the bridge
and beyond the trees of the park
on the other side of the river waves.
The tricolor has just been hoisted on the boat
on this side of the bridge.
As I now recall the painting,
the colors are summer bright, almost "joyful."
Therefore, the silhouette of the shadowy dark lady
becomes increasingly blacker—
as if epitomizing
absence itself against the sky.
The entire pain of leave-taking is in her gesture.
How deeply loss has been anticipated here!
But since we see her against the light
it is impossible to say if she is turning her back to us
or if she's turning toward us:
if she's looking off to the southwest
sunlight is falling on her face
(which we are never going to see);
if she is turned toward us, it is in the shadow
(and we can only imagine her features).
In other words, we do not know
if her gaze is turned in the same direction as ours
and she is raising her hand to greet
someone who is disappearing down the river
or if it is we who are now disappearing upstream
and receive her greeting.
We see her for the last time.

But conversely it is equally possible
that it is we who are approaching her
while traveling downstream.
As if we have been apart for years
and are at long last returning. (How pleased she is to see us again!)
Finally it is of course also possible
that we are witnessing someone else's return
—the way she sees it, from a point far behind her—
and that the old world here is being
shipped back upstream, and I
suddenly find that I am waving,
waving like her, waving
to someone I once loved, to the days
that are now gloriously returning upstream in the late sun,
maybe by a barge, whose tricolor has been hoisted:
everything has been exempted from duty
in this golden hour.
But I will never ever see
the features of her face as she waves from her bridge,
waves, waves incessantly,
I will never ever know
if this is a farewell
or a return,
nor whose farewell or return
the painting is about.
For a moment the picture seems to beam
with all its possibilities:
it becomes at once a homecoming and a farewell.
And the woman is brightly shining darkness.
It is an afternoon
almost a century ago.
The sky a golden ground beyond the bridge.

THE VILLA DORIA PAMPHILI

We often made the parks of Rome our refuge.
Most of all the Borghese Park with its oaks and pines
and the little open-air cafe by the pond
in whose shade we would drink mineral water
on hot summer days;
in a shadowy room of the palace
hung the largest of Titian's paintings
which in spite of darkened colors
and its need of restoration
made its content shine:
L'amore sacro e l'amore profano.
The sound of its water follows us still.
On certain Sundays we would even go to the Villa Ada,
dry afternoons when the sand
blew in the light and the grass among the pines
was completely yellow: the families,
sad and dressed in black, would walk
to and fro while making conversation.
But on this day we were neither with Titian
nor in the metaphysical dryness of the Villa Ada.
We had taken the bus across the Tiber
to explore the Villa Doria Pamphili,
a huge park just south of the Vatican.
The palace of the same name
we had already visited:
a museum in which painting after painting
was an inner Arcadia to us.
Here we were in the outer world.
The afternoon was sunny, no rain was expected.
The limestone walls seemed to have cracked from heat and dryness.
But if the lawn here had yellowed
there was green grass in the shade of the trees.
That's where the families were! The father

stretched out with a transistor radio by his ear,
the mother who had just opened up the picnic basket,
the son who had grown tired of football . . .
Surely his sister was now
in the shadows deeper under the trees,
perhaps with his grandmother and aunt . . .
But I only really remember Massimo,
as childishly fat as his name.
We had settled down nearby to get some rest.
You spent a lot of time those days with Dante,
whom you were reading for pleasure . . .
perhaps to revisit a time in your life
when you studied the *Commedia* at school.
You knew Italian. I was envying you the ease
with which you traveled
through the geography of hell
when I suddenly noticed
that smoke as from the burning tires of cars
filled the entire sky to the north.
That way the park is bounded by the ancient Via Aurelia.
Somewhere farther off
a considerable fire was in progress
but in our minds it was as if hell itself had erupted.
The smoke was an impenetrable bluish black.
The park with its families
suddenly became movingly terrestrial:
a "paradise" in the etymological sense—
with shades of freshness among the trees
and you by my side.
I knew that our earthly paradise
was doomed to destruction;
and yet this fact made the colors under the trees
shine yet more intensely in their obscurity.
We began to sense the smell of smoke, not strongly
because that day there was probably a faint westerly wind.

I widened my nostrils:
yes, those were car tires burning
at a place fairly high up in hell.
We stood up the better to see what was going on.
While we were watching the smoke belching out
a whiff of wind
came from the west
dispersing the curtain of smoke for a moment
and allowing us to see as in a vision
the cupola of St. Peter's—
shining in its whiteness
like a marble sky in the sky.

AT THE PORTA DEL POPOLO

At the beginning of this century Rilke lived in Rome
and must quite often have passed through the Porta del Popolo
to get to the center of town—
and then back again under the same arch
on his way to the Via Flaminia;
it was there he had his apartment.
These circumstances make it possible
to attribute to his "Roman Sarcophagi"
an almost literal meaning:
when you are standing on the Piazza del Popolo
looking northward toward the gray facade of the town gate
there is on either side
an ancient marble coffin
where the water is constantly streaming down
from the iron pipes in the wall.—In summer
early in the wet afternoon
when shadows were beginning to fall over the one to the left
but when the one to the right was still exposed to the dazzling sun
shining also on the broad steps of Santa Maria del Popolo
at the time when the buses came thundering in
under the big arch in the middle,
we used to stop in order to drink: with your thumb
you would choke the aperture of the curved iron pipe
making the water spurt right up in a jet
from a little hole just above. Ah!
There were many people dressed in white summer clothes
who would bow forward and drink.
It would often happen that we then went on
toward the left, exterior side arch of the gate
with its shady bookshop
and the florist who had his stand
just around the corner as you came out:
bouquets in green plastic buckets,

buckets and cans on springy planks,
brass faucets and hoses,
flowers in vases, brimming over with water—
in the shade of the same gate.
The asphalt of the sidewalk was shining wet.
In the town plan of my memory the florist's is now
the "symmetrical inversion" of the sarcophagus.
The florist's in shadow, the sarcophagus in sunshine . . .
The florist's in the north, the sarcophagus in the south . . .
But both were situated to the right
as you entered through the gate
from the north and the south respectively.
We were standing at the threshold of the Eternal City.
You were buying white or red carnations.
But to you a carnation had nothing to do with death:
it was a pure explosion of joy;
and I felt that it was true—
while I continued to think of the water we had drunk.
For in Rilke's poem the sarcophagus now seemed
to be an allegory of the poem itself,
now that its author was gone. The objects
that had once been put in the coffin
in whose darkness they must have glimmered
disappeared without a trace together with the corpse,
shrouded in its rotting clothes.
And permitted the last stanza of the poem,
whose content had now been emptied,
to become completely transparent:
shimmering moments of a language—
when the water from the aqueducts of antiquity
at long last had rushed in.

AT THE GRAVE OF C. F. HILL

Often I would walk the shady path
that divides the dense foliage of the Botanical Gardens
from the East Cemetery in the north.
It never occurred to me that Carl Fredrik Hill was buried
just inside the railing of the graveyard.
But today I am out of the shade.
I am standing here beside the grave.
The stone with its inscription is turned to the east—
as if to greet the sun
when at dawn it proclaims
that the world is new.
Moist tree trunks are gleaming everywhere.
But the sun is mercilessly rising;
and the sun is his Father
whose gaze it is impossible to meet.
At noon the streets of the city are empty.
Brick walls are gleaming, hot,
and single chestnut trees cast shadows
clearly outlined on the earth and cobblestones.
No one leaves the smaller houses.
(In the gardens dim villas can be glimpsed.)
And here, in the depth of the cemetery,
among the countless others are the shades of sisters—
two who meekly, tenderly,
attend to a shadowy brother
in the Parental Home under the earth.
Loving shades of these two sisters underground . . .
Although foliage obscures them
one can guess their presence in their brother's final room.
Deep is the shadow that is open
to the underworld . . .
Then the dusk comes down with all its freshness.
Silver-plated, verdure is reflected in his window.

Verandas, voices, white garden furniture . . .
He beholds but a reflection
of the feverish sights of the sunset:
immense clouds have gathered in the east
illuminated by the evening sun—
and this is his heavenly kingdom,
the vast kingdom of his dreams—
realms, prospects, colonnades, and snowy mountains
resting in a luminous distance . . .
How far from us the living
in the green depths of the earth!
And while the evening down here grows more dense
he finds comfort in the thought
that high up there among the silent clouds
—golden, sunlit—
it is always afternoon, Olympian,
streaming with light.

V

TRANSTRÖMER EPIGONES

As to the question of "the Tranströmer epigones,"
the origin of the phenomenon—
that is to say Tomas Tranströmer himself—
has, according to my source,
always been most skeptical and
even doubted the existence of such youths.
With a single exception:
sometime soon after 1960
he received a letter from me including a poem
that was "pure plagiarism."
What a humiliation!
In vain have I searched through old manuscripts
in the hope of finding
at least a draft of the poem
which I remember fairly well:
graphically, it imitated the form of "Weather Picture."
With a drumming all the apples fell to the ground!
I established in the first line of the poem
that the wind blew so strongly on that autumn day
there were white horses on the sea—
heedless of the fact that every wave
on the black-green sea all the way to Tuborg
was whinnying in protest at my image!
The ferry services were cancelled . . .
The roof tiles whistled,
empty tree crowns boomed,
newspapers and leaves blew eastward,
and the whole town seemed to take off and ascend
while I, as Tranströmer's one true epigone,
fighting a muscular headwind,
struggled westward along the pond
getting closer to my piano lesson
step by step.

HISTORY

The first time I ever saw a Negro was in January 1953
near Sture's bicycle shop in Landskrona
where Föreningsgatan runs into Östra Infartsgatan.
While earlier I had seen black people only in photographs,
now a living Negro came walking down the street!
His face shone like mahogany in the sun.
At the time I was with my grandmother, a fact that now
so many years later I find significant: in the summer of 1903
when she was nearly twenty, she foundered
on a Swedish freighter that had collided in the Thames—
it was early in the morning and my grandmother,
who could not swim, was pulled to shore by a Negro.
There she stood in her nightgown just before sunrise.
London was waking up. That moment marked the birth
of her confidence in "the Negroes":
it was, of course, to them she owed her life!
Even as an octogenarian she had a passion, for example, for Josh White,
the blues singer of the dazzling surname:
every time he appeared on television
she would watch admiringly how beads of sweat
stood out on his forehead. Meanwhile, I had started
listening to jazz myself and would spend all my money on records:
to help me reorganize my finances
she made a point of buying *Orkester-Journalen,*
perhaps because she unconsciously
identified it with "the music of the blacks,"
making the price of a single copy a monthly installment
on her life's debt. In one issue
I read to her how Charlie Parker,
touring Sweden with his band,
needed water for his radiator one summer night
and so stopped at a farm.
Brought up herself on a farm, she listened attentively:

the farmer who was in the habit of feeding music to his cows
because he thought that that would make them milk the better
asked the musicians for a service in return
and then switched on his primitive recorder in the barn . . .
The track had been recovered and would be released!
The July night was enchanted all around us.
In the distance a milk cow dreamed about "the Bird,"
bellowing with pleasure in the middle of its dream.

—FOR DONALD BILLINGSLEY

THE X

The weeks before I left the army
life itself seemed about to break its camp:
Stockholm a magnificent and thawing chaos
that was both an outer
and an inner reality . . . For the first time
I felt, on that Saturday in March,
an inkling of liberty,
conversely proportional
to the last ten months' coercion:
about eleven or twelve I must have
stopped in the crowd by the crossing
at Sveavägen and Kungsgatan
waiting for the light to turn green—
when I discovered
on the opposite sidewalk
beyond the cars and groaning buses
Sven "the X" Erixon
recognizable from a photograph.
He was tall, bareheaded, wore a long brown overcoat
and seemed to be in excellent spirits.
Consequently the light turned green.
In the midst of those about to pass me
he came walking straight in my direction,
actually staring at me
as though he wanted to catch my attention.
Just before he passed me in the sleet
he cried triumphantly:
"The car horns sound exactly like trumpets!"
While the remark was not directed at anybody with him
but more or less at all of us who just that moment
were crossing Sveavägen,
it was somehow understood that precisely I
should be the one to remember those words:

"They might come in handy in a poem."
This must have been what he had in mind.
How each of them glimmered in the sun
on that blaring springlike winter's day!
I felt the melting snow inside my shoes.
Far away extended big and silent city blocks
whose yards were full of shade.
For a couple of weeks
the whole world had been on the verge of breaking camp.

—FOR BENGT-ÅKE SANDSTRÖM

SYNTAGMA

About the distinction that linguists make
between syntagm and paradigm
(and the troublesome difference that exists
as to their definition)
we didn't have the slightest clue:
but there we were, no doubt about it,
one of the last days of June 1964
on Syntagma in Athens, reading a Swedish paper
reporting on how Midsummer celebrations
had turned out. Among other things,
one article described how an inebriated man at night
had walked down to the bank of a Lapland river
where he had discovered a steel wire
stretching across the rushing waters:
hanging by his arms, he had managed to get to the middle
where the stream is at its swiftest
and the roar had as it were shut him into its room.
He was hanging in his own turbulent silence.
The fire brigade had been alarmed.
They were standing on the bank, shouting and trying
to make him see reason: he didn't hear a word!
The gnats must have been dancing by the river.
Presumably, it was impossible
to row out in a boat and save him by that means.
What was to be done to lure him back?
I have forgotten how the article ends.
(In front of the sentry boxes of the Royal Palace
the soldiers suddenly present arms.)
Therefore, in my memory the man is still hanging there
right over the most turbulent part of the stream
while firemen stand on the bank
trying in agitated voices to find a solution
to the hanging man's dilemma.

What *was* his problem? Perhaps
he had no other answer to his metaphysical questions
than to hang there by his arms
while using up all his muscular strength.
Perhaps he had come to an impasse
in some discussion he'd had with himself or with God.
Perhaps he had suddenly found it impossible
to "make things cohere."
The article about him could not have an end
since his inner discussion was as yet unfinished.
Big fir trees were standing serious and silent
between the road and the river bank.
But the sun was ready to be the sun again just above the horizon:
it had hardly disappeared before it rose once more.
It shot traces of light through enormous fog banks.
The dew was glittering in a cobweb
stretched across the path.
The world seemed to shine with a shimmering
belonging only to fairy tales . . .
The music from the dance floor of the people's park
must have fallen silent by now:
the band members had probably left
while the gnats continued the dance
and the number of people on the bank grew and grew.
There must have been a crowd.
They are standing there in silence, wondering what will happen.
And the man himself is hanging by the steel wire,
hanging by his strong, northern arms
over the most turbulent stream of the river.
Thirty years later I realize
that such a moment is "paradigmatic."

TOURIST PEOPLE

Up and down the central mountain ridge in Crete
we rode the bus due south from Iraklion.
Vineyards, olive groves, and fig trees
all resembled rows of ideograms
impressed in the dried clay of landscape.
On the right Mount Ida where Zeus himself was born.
Because the Cyprus conflict, May of 1964,
had stemmed the flow of tourists
we seemed to our surprise the only ones
at Phaestos needing any help from Alexandros.
He wore the kingdom's emblem on his gray peaked cap.
When he saw that we were reading the *Blue Guide*
he took my copy and turned at once to the place
where he was mentioned with the views—
Henry Miller's description of him had made him famous!
As if by habit, he took a ballpoint pen and changed
"A. Miller" to "H. Miller" in my book.
The heat made even the stairs seem to tremble.
The scent of pine was overwhelming.
"Came rain, came wind, came tourist people here!"
he exclaimed, trying to explain
why so little was left of the palace.
His words echoed oddly in the calm.
Four of them might very well
have come from Pindar
who in his sixth Pythian Ode describes
how rain and wind lay waste the proudest monuments.
The rain and wind. Not the other way around!
As for "the tourists," they were there all right:
just two that day who step by step
wore down the stones a little thinner on the floor.

THE SOCRATIC PROBLEM

Down on earth the olive trees stood up arrayed for war,
an old man pottered in his vineyard,
wheat fields were already green—
and from a window we saw Attica
spreading out below us.
We were sitting in a dazzling lecture hall
high among the clouds.
In my imagination I could see Professor Havelock
excited by our statistical surveys
walking back and forth in the world of ideas.
Myself, I'd been assigned the task of counting out
reflexive pronouns in the plays of Aristophanes
and had barely gotten through *The Clouds*
where the frequency of "myself," "yourself," "itself"
not so unexpectedly had risen up
to quite Olympic heights.
Reflexive pronouns!
When the cloudy form of Socrates appeared
the many little mirrors of morphology shone out,
the silver owls blinked,
and sun beamed down on white frost and the dew.
Ironic reflections there converged in points of light
even in the middle of the day.
Had Plato modeled his doctrine of ideas
on *The Clouds* of Aristophanes?
A syntactical storm
built up darkly on the far horizon.
The old man who was working in his vineyard
nervously lifted his gaze:
it was heading straight in his direction!
The Acropolis was in shade
and Eric Havelock had disappeared.
I stood alone, waiting for the wind and pelting rain.

THE MISTRESS

In a dry and oddly piercing voice
Jean Genet read out his text.
He had come to the U.S.A.
to offer the Black Panther Party his support
as the Bobby Seale trial approached.
It was a chilly morning in March.
He seemed small and sallow
sitting there before the TV camera at a conference table
of a cozy common room
at Yale University.
The glare of the TV lights was strong.
The two Panther leaders sitting on his right
listened inscrutably
as the female interpreter
translated every sentence into English.
She was Genet's compatriot:
didn't she have unusually glittering eyes?
For almost a month
she would faithfully accompany him
while he delivered the same message
to large audiences on the East Coast:
freedom to Bobby Seale, freedom to all political prisoners!
After a well-attended rally at Yale
at which hundreds of dollars had been earned
for the party's trial fund
Genet appeared alone onstage
as though he were waiting for the last attendants to leave.
The organizers seemed a little worried:
all the takings had disappeared!
Who on earth could have stolen them?
Indefatigable, they kept on searching . . .
until the Thief, grinning, handed back his spoils:
the old master demonstrated

that indeed he knew the art of theft!
While news of his prank made the others laugh
a college student pointed
shyly to the beautiful interpreter
—who three years later would become my lawful wife—
and asked in a quivering voice:
"Is that Jean Genet's mistress?"

LA MER

Once in a while our table conversation might
concern the perception of the sea in Charles Trénet's "La Mer"
which was recorded in the mid-forties.
I myself had grown up by an entirely different sea
but seemed to share
a sea that was not mine but yours:
I suggested that our perception
was determined by "a certain way of filming the sea"
which we associate with the forties—
black and white, of course, but above all
with slow, almost dawdling reflections of the sun,
single, slowly twinkling silver flashes
in the sea shot looking south,
in the sea at noon.
Black shadows in the foreground—
they make the soundless play of the sun
seem even more dazzling out at sea.
It is as if these dawdling reflections had given me access
to a world that was not mine—
for a moment I really believe
that communication is possible,
that the images have an inner life to convey,
see you on the Mediterranean beach:
the periphery is blurred but in the middle of the picture
the definition is so strong
that I see the glitter in the little girl's eyes
where she stands in the glittering waves,
where she is overcome by the sea today,
by merely existing near a summer sea,
where without a doubt she hears voices shouting
though she cannot make out what they are saying in the surge
—while the clouds imperceptibly have come to a halt
in the depth of the clearest of bays.

THE SUITCASES

In the eyes of the Vichy regime your father was a "Bolshevik"
which may have contributed
to his being drafted for a work-service unit
to be forwarded to Nazi Germany.
On this beautiful October day, 1942, just outside Algiers
he was at any rate sweeping barracks
where he had been interned until further notice—
when suddenly he discovered a senior officer
with two heavy suitcases
on his way out. It is still morning in memory.
In the barrack square it is cool.
Your father who is seventeen
has put away the broom
and politely asks the colonel
if he needs assistance with his bags.
He receives a highly appreciative answer,
grabs the shining leather cases
and then follows diagonally behind—
out past the guard. What time is it?
Perhaps ten-thirty. It is very hot out there.
The strong North African sun
shines over the landscape
as they walk up the dirt road
past a scorched area as large as a soccer field.
What a lot of dust there is on the road!
A little farther away stands a flock of sheep.
The colonel has other matters on his mind
and doesn't say a word during the walk.
The young man behind him,
slackening his pace,
sweat dripping from his forehead,
pauses under a tree, puts the suitcases down
as if to get a better grip . . .

His gaze is completely still in the shade.
The colonel has doubtless heard
the scratching of the suitcases against the dirt
but doesn't react—not until the boy
is running like a sprinter after the starting shot
and already out in the light
and disappearing quickly in the bushes.
Reluctant to leave the suitcases unattended on the road
the colonel watches him escape.
Nothing for it but to carry them from this point on himself.
A bleating is heard in the story.
Rommel is still undefeated in Libya.
One year later your father is standing
in a British uniform on a ship bound for Liverpool.

AT ST. LARS'S

If memory serves, I was visiting an American deserter
who had been committed to St. Lars's
one April evening early in the 1970s—
they had given him so many sedatives
that after five minutes
with heavy eyelids and a drawling voice
he asked me to leave, exhausted . . .
I suppose I must have been on my way out
of the big old-fashioned hospital building
and had stopped in a hall
where a broad flight of stairs in the middle
created two separate levels:
mumbling patients sat scattered around all over,
you heard the clatter of trays,
nurses dressed in white
walked up and down in clogs appearing and disappearing . . .
White-painted doors and panels, potted plants, tables . . .
The low sun beamed into the hall
filling it with an inexplicable light
when a man in his forties—
big, rather tanned,
wearing a jacket and a flannel shirt—
came walking briskly down the stairs,
singing with a singular conviction: "Wheresoe'er I go
in woods, mountains, and valleys
a friend goes with me, and I hear his voice!"
The space around his words was enormous.
He looked me straight in the eye
as if he knew me well.
God must have just descended at St. Lars's.
Were we the only ones who had noticed?
He sang with great certainty—
as if the moment

could have turned out only just this way.
His mind was a teeming revival meeting.
Far off in their separate worlds the patients seemed to pray.
The big common room
flamed intensely in its sun.
Corridors led far out into solitude.

IN MEMORIAM K.A.

I first came to Athens in May of 1964:
the train wheeled slowly into the station
in such a strong and vertical Mediterranean light
that I thought I must have arrived in the Middle East
rather than Europe: somewhere
I had read the word *sidēródromos,* which means "railroad";
it is composed of two elements
meaning "iron" and "road"
that I recognized at once from Homer.
Homer! I stood by an abyss in time,
the strong sunlight made the station building hover in the air.
Much later we used to sit in your office
and prepare ourselves for seminars
on the epigrams of the Greek Anthology.
One of them made me think of that May day in 1964;
the poet's name was Alcaeus of Messene
and the poem was an epitaph on a celebrated actor.
In the last line, it says that the deceased
had taken "the iron road" to Hades.
The road down there is certainly inexorable and hard . . .
Thus, an iron road. Literally, it says:
"You took the iron road to the Kingdom of the Dead."
I remember how you laughed at this abyss
in the Greek language, laughed
at this magnificent absurd coincidence
so that there was a long echo in the stone staircase of the college
from the cellar right up to the ceiling.
Since then you have yourself taken the railroad down to Hades.
But when I think of your journey
it is not the realm of the shades that comes to mind
but the railroad station in Athens:
the year is 1964 and the building hovers still
in the shimmering Mediterranean light.

MENELAOS ON PHAROS

Things had been violent in the *Iliad* that night.
A considerable number of heroes
had tumbled wheezing onto the ground
on account of Helen . . .
How many deaths! Homer was indefatigable
in his copious descriptions of wounds:
now a lance drove to the root of somebody's nose,
now a hero was slashed by a sword in the gut
so that his bowels poured out—
"and night shrouded his eyes."
The table lamp trembled
like a seismograph during a distant earthquake
where we were sitting on the fifth floor
in an otherwise totally dark apartment:
the text open before us,
grammar and dictionary within easy reach,
the table a square gambling table covered with a classically green felt.
It must have been in the late winter of '75.
Jon Bordo had been busy studying the *Iliad*
but needed some help here and there
in the identification, for example, of troublesome verb forms . . .
It must have been around eleven at night
when my wife suddenly
ran into the room and exclaimed
like a messenger in a Greek play: "The staircase is covered with blood!"
We had just finished our assignment
and were quite taken aback for a moment:
in our minds, it was the blood of heroes that streamed . . .
We had heard nothing at all.
The landlady stood on the landing down there
repeating like mad:
"Don't wipe away any blood, there will be a police inquiry!"
Her tenants in the apartment below

were a blonde waitress and a man
who filleted fish in the Halles
and would therefore often be away at night.
You could meet him on the stairs
when large and silent
he returned early in the morning.
He must have had a good hand with the knife
with which he cut up
newly caught fish from three different seas:
the North Sea, the Atlantic, and the Mediterranean.
Tons of fresh fish in cases,
bodies blank with slime,
dead staring eyes. Crushed ice . . .
His wife worked at a restaurant on the block.
"What an exceptionally good figure," I would think
when I saw her through the restaurant window
dressed in a white blouse and a black skirt
with a white, coquettishly small lace apron.
She would work late too—
but some nights she was free.
This very night her husband had come home unexpectedly
and found her in bed
with a stranger . . .
Since this poem to some extent
wishes to observe the rule of the unity of space
I leave it up to the reader to imagine the scene
the moment before the husband
opened the door of the apartment . . .
In the knife fight that ensued
he drove his rival, half dressed and bloody,
down the winding stairs; his wife had imperceptibly
disappeared from the scene of the battle.
And left her husband alone . . .
Life went back to normal.
Certain mornings in early summer he would fry fish in his kitchen

like Menelaos on Pharos
and the wind carried the smell up to our window
which was open toward the backyard . . .
The church clock on the island struck seven.
Now and then you would hear his china and cutlery
clink in the silence as he ate.

FRASCATI

During a certain period our friend Valentino
was of the decided opinion
that a rational account could be made of life
except on one single point: wine
was something so extraordinary
that its existence must be due to divine
intervention in the world.
This was what he referred to as his "theology."
The cupola of St. Peter's
was shining in the sun.
No doubt we were talking about this
sitting opposite each other reading the menu
at the restaurant in Frascati:
a white cloth on our table, heavy shining knives and forks,
large glasses for water and wine,
thick napkins, fragrant
as though fresh from the mangle . . .
Although for this time of day it was hot outside
the restaurant was cool:
was it the stone floor that breathed its hoarded cold?
A big carafe of white wine was brought in.
In the morning we had paid a visit
to the Villa Aldobrandini on the slopes above.
Although the villa itself was dilapidated
G. J. Adlerbeth's 1784 description
still seemed to us quite accurate:
"Right before the main building
is a constantly surging cascade
like a theater of stone, full of water pipes,
which, when the water is running, causes a rumble
similar to that of thunder . . ." For at any moment
the water might make the stone orchestra intone!
In the park you stand photographed

wearing a green summer dress with a floral pattern
at the entrance of a grotto
which is the Cyclops's mouth:
the heat from the park above
is broken against the green coolness of your back
causing a prismatic phenomenon in memory—
shimmering green lights
as in the greenest of all green poems.
The Frascati wine was on our table,
sparkling in a sunbeam.
As I remember its transparency, so many years later,
it changed our vision completely:
our myopia disappeared,
your myopia and mine
—which is considerably stronger—
and at a distance of "twelve Italian miles"
we could clearly perceive
the smallest tile
on the sunlit roofs down in Rome.

EXPLODED HAIKU

We must have been talking about Lindegren's late poems
while the bus took us along the Tiber
at great speed—
we had been down on the Isola Tiberina
which with its decaying walls, its verdure and healing power,
seemed to us like an emblem
of his life: the almost completely demolished bridge,
the Ponte Rotto, which you can see from the island,
suggesting some catastrophe had occurred . . .
Lindegren had visited Rome in April 1967.
The Man without a Way became
a Don Quixote in the poem he wrote,
the "exploded sonnet"
having been restored with care
and yet appearing incomplete.
Its masonry was in a state of quiet disrepair.
Standing in the crowded bus, we
now and then were thrown off balance
as it rushed beside the plane trees by the Tiber
and came to a halt with a sudden jerk
at a stop: a man
stepped on the bus and stood quite near us.
Ammazza! He was an exact copy of Erik Lindegren,
only eight or ten sizes smaller,
the top of his head reaching our shoulders at most.
The same slanted eyes, the same feline heaviness.
We both must have been struck by the resemblance,
for suddenly it was as if we said in one voice:
"Exploded haiku!" Irresistibly
laughter bubbled up in us: seconds later
we quickly jumped from the bus
and, no longer trying to restrain ourselves,
let it explode by the Tiber.

THE WATER HEATER

A water heater had been installed by the bathtub
in the apartment we were renting:
since its thermostat was out of order
our landlord had advised us
just to turn off the electricity at night
and turn it on again in the morning.
For more than a year this system worked
and we lived with it as a matter of course
making no attempt at repairs.
Now you tell me that it was during a walk in the Meudon woods
on one of the last days of the 1970s
that we in one terrifying moment
realized that we hadn't switched off the current as usual—
which was why we immediately walked home.
The big metal cylinder
might detonate at any moment!
I rushed into the bathroom and managed to press the button.
We heaved a sigh of relief . . .
In order to evacuate the water
which by now had certainly reached the boiling point
I turned on the warm water faucet.
What a surprise
when a jet of boiling steam spurted out—
as from a wheezing and coughing jet engine!
The faucet's mouth kept puffing for a while . . .
My reflection in the bathroom mirror disappeared.
Lightbulbs shone like pale suns in the mist.
Eventually the corridor outside
and the adjacent rooms
were filled with warm, shapeless steam
in which we wandered about for the rest of the evening.
Some years later
I disembarked at Naples harbor

where I had come from Capri.
The water was lapping, visibility was good.
I was to teach a class at eleven o'clock.
On the wharf I discovered that a crowd
had gathered in the sunshine around a newspaper stand
and wondered what was going on—
people stood silent before the front page of a daily
pasted up like a placard:
"The government coalition
finally has blown up," the headline said.
The photo which covered most of the page
showed what remained
of Montecitorio Palace in Rome:
the chamber of deputies had been blown up!
The only thing remaining was really
an immense crater bounded
by the exterior contour of the palace foundations.
What had happened?
It was not a terrorist attack.
The newspaper text explained
that "a water heater had exploded in the cellar."
I thought of course of our own experience
and believed what I read—
as if a water heater were capable of exploding
with the strength of a blockbuster.
Once again the steam was dense.
Among those who were gaping with surprise
studying the "news" in front of the stand
I spotted one of my best students,
as gullible as I was.
Foghorns seemed to reverberate
across all of Naples Bay.

SANTA MARINELLA

As you approach Rome from the north by train,
Santa Marinella is the last station
to whistle by: you catch a glimpse of the yellow station house,
palms, magnolias, assorted seaside buildings
and then for a little while the main road
softly following the bay—
perhaps a few swimmers,
a ball on the water, bathing caps, parasols.
But I never got to Santa Marinella in the summer.
Only in winter! One Sunday in pouring rain
we arrived by bus
and sat in a cold apartment
that the electric fire
couldn't manage to heat.
Brrr . . . We went out in the rain
and bought some fresh-caught fish and small mussels:
here were fishes I had seen only a few times before,
red mullet, bass, shimmering sepias . . .
About an hour later we had a steaming dish
of *spaghetti alle vongole*
on our table.—The whole afternoon
the Tyrrhenic Sea was running high
over the asphalt road,
was flooding it while the rain poured down, leaving
sea urchins on it as it sucked back gravel
into the depth. Not a single parasol was to be seen,
cafés and restaurants were closed.
Antonio told us about a house nearby
whose construction had been interrupted
in the absence of a building permit.
The architect had placed the toilet
in the middle of the ground floor
but though the house was several stories high

the bathroom had no ceiling. Madness!
In the evening when the rain had moved away
we went to have a look at it.
In the roped-off area police
had placed a sign: *VIETATO L'INGRESSO.* We entered.
The stairs and walls were naked concrete.
The vegetation had begun its slow invasion:
the building was already a Roman ruin . . .
But as we stood there in the space
that had obviously been intended as a privy
our gazes were drawn toward the ceiling:
like a great telescope the room continued
several stories up into the darkness.
Slowly the stars revolved
up there in the universe.

ON LEARNING THAT THE SANTO BAMBINO DI ARACOELI HAS FINALLY BEEN STOLEN BY THE MAFIA

The whole week the noise of their bagpipes
had been heard in lanes and on piazzas:
clad in dirty sheepskin *i pifferai* had descended
from the rough valleys of the Abruzzi
to make a buck in the Christmas trade.
Snowless winter days in Rome. The evening sun
lent a warm tone to cupolas and towers
and made the ochre facades of the houses glow.
The windowpanes were ablaze.
Farther down, in the shade,
the street was an endless swarm of people . . .
At the stands of Piazza Navona
they were selling manger figures until the last moment:
here were light-blue Marias, asses and brown oxen,
cribs, a graying Joseph,
grazing ewes, small white lambs,
and of course bagpipe-playing shepherds,
identical to those we heard in the streets.
Here they were lined up in a silent miniature world,
pious and expressionless
in the light of strong lamps.
People were thronging and buzzing,
shooting and buying nougat.
It was cold and clear. There was a rumor
that the Mafia were intending to steal
the Santo Bambino from the Aracoeli church on the Capitol.
We took it to be a joke
intended to create drama around the Christmas mass; and the perspective
did create excitement in the church
to which we had gone that evening
together with some friends.
It was so crowded that there was barely room for us.

The Christ child in question was a life-size sculpture,
carved of olive wood from Gethsemane, no less:
it was coated with gold and set with precious jewels.
The picture of the Child that I had carried
in my wallet for twenty years
told me that the artist was a Franciscan monk
at work in the fifteenth century.
Exactly at midnight the excitement reached its height.
Suddenly there was a sigh of relief
through those assembled:
escorted by police, the Santo Bambino was carried
up the long aisle
and seemed positively to shine
"with the holy fire which it had brought into the world."
We could not see how it was put in the manger.
But the Christmas night was illuminated
by its precious stones and gold—
or was it the stars twinkling high up there
in the friendly sky?
The shepherds out in the fields
blew their bagpipes,
their shrill notes sounding far around.
Floating angels
might have sung on high.

SORA CECILIA

On the metal curtains that had been pulled down
in front of the restaurant's door and window
it might as well have said "Closed for vacation" or "Closed on Sundays."
We would have been patient enough
and returned another time.
We are standing at the corner of Via Poli and Via del Bufalo.
The restaurant has closed for good.
The premises have been empty for a long time, a neighbor explains,
and there's probably nothing left of the furnishings
in the shadows behind the gray curtains
even though the floor, the walls, the doors, and the ceiling
must still be the same—
the final tangible parameters of our memory
in the darkness. The rooms seem irretrievably lost in the past—
I am put in mind
how one February day while crossing Rome
when sunlight fell through foliage of plane trees
along the streets and in expansive parks
I had the presence of mind to go to Sora Cecilia,
as if I had realized that I would never get
another chance. Deep down there among facades of houses
the daylight was only indirect:
winter sun reflected in the windowpanes and mirrors.
Blue and green reflections, the presence
of trembling water surfaces, plenty of customers inside,
a strangely exhilarating atmosphere,
and a little table with a white cloth
which seemed to be reserved for me.
A smell as of rime: it was as cold indoors
as on the shady winter streets
yet all the regulars seemed perfectly happy
to be sitting there in their outdoor clothes.
The plane trees had lost their leaves.

The sun fell through strong branches.
"Che facciamo oggi?" asked signor Luciano
in the lively dimness of the restaurant.
Impeccable in his white jacket, mustachioed,
with his order pad in hand
as if he were awaiting
a signal for the creation of the world.
I knew that the kitchen opened up at the very back
and thought of its big saucepans,
of heavy, boiling pots under cool vaults,
of clouds of steam, heat and cold,
the murmur of shimmering table water,
mist, and the unfathomable depth of the mirrors.
The house minestrone seemed to be made of certain vocables
derived from the luxuriant garden plot of the Italian language:
potatoes, carrots, and zucchini that the cook
had cut into cubes at her table,
onions, white beets and tomatoes, tender string beans,
shredded lettuce leaves, perhaps white cabbage
and a kind of macaroni, cannolicchi,
which was added at the end of the boiling,
absorbed water and swelled.
I see her sitting out there at her table:
she cuts quickly and carefully, shredding and slicing . . .
When Luciano comes in with my steaming minestrone
the grated cheese is already there on my table
in its cylinder of metal and glass.
Cosmological thought:
against the dryness and drought of winter
stands the splashing, hot soup in my bowl!
I am sitting in front of a garden kitchen
that has simmered in the pot on a winter's day
and feel in my hand the weight of the soupspoon.
"E poi, che facciamo?" What a question!
As if it were already the second day of creation!

And while I am waiting for the main course
it seems as if this very moment
enclosed the memory of another visit
to the same deep and shimmering premises.
And that this in turn encompasses yet another—
perhaps a late autumn night when the city
was dark and cold, solitary voices echoed
farther away in the block, a door
slammed shut with a desolate sound; and suddenly
the illuminated warmth of the restaurant,
the plates of antipasti and fruits,
the white-laid tables and—
"Che facciamo stasera?"
The wine from Grottaferrata stood in its carafe
like a lighthouse on the table,
heavy and transparent.
We were treated to a lesson in the variant
of Italian spoken in Rome:
sora does not mean "sister," as you might have thought,
but is a contraction of the word *signora*—
the name simply means
"Restaurant Mother Cecilia,"
someone sitting next to us explained.
And in its turn this quiet evening
contained yet another evening;
and so on. As if every visit
to Restaurant Sora Cecilia were the successful
repetition of a previous one!
Until we finally get back
to our first, mythical Meal—
which doesn't necessarily contain another memory
except the Idea of the Table, the Idea of Table Community,
the rectangular Idea of the Tablecloth . . .
The whiteness of the tablecloth was indeed Olympian.
It beamed on your face.

You were smiling. We were newly married.
And Luciano in white, like a god:
"Che facciamo oggi?" We seemed to be gazing at the Idea of the Menu . . .
But at that very moment some water hit
a red-hot cast-iron range in the kitchen
giving rise to immense clouds of steam
behind which a wonderful wedding now took place:
pots were boiling, drops of condensation running
along the ceiling and the walls—
here were faucets and colanders, metal ladles, barrels,
iron ranges, oven doors, forks and spits;
flames of fire burning, flames of fire scorching—
but in particular the steam
of such excessive quantity
that it is still pouring forth out of my memory,
formless and puffing, from the innermost regions of memory
where the male and female cooks both appear from time to time,
the world shimmering like a colossal minestrone,
and your face beaming across the tablecloth—
yes, we are newly married, we walk out into the light
and when we are standing on the pavement outside the door
it is early afternoon and spring:
the sun is warm, the leaves of the plane trees
are just beginning to burst
and there is a murmur of people in the streets.

THE PEDESTAL

Although our bus had left Athens
I couldn't stop thinking about Phrasikleia's pedestal.
Black, almost illegible,
like a stupendous meteor
hurled to us from the very kingdom of the dead,
it had filled me with unease:
the heavy stone block seemed to radiate a darkness
now that it had finally taken its place
under the inevitable kore.
For the first time I had now seen the statue
that had pursued me for years,
recognized its epigram in the scratched threadbare stone
and established that Phrasikleia
was larger than me.
I was smaller than Phrasikleia.
I explained to my son
that his grandfather had read the inscription around 1930
in Pontén's old primer
and noticed the alliteration on the K:
koúrē keklḗsomai aieí ΚΟΡΕΚΕΚΛΕΣΟΜΑΙΑΙΕΙ,
"henceforth I shall always be called daughter."
The K seemed to hold back a current of air.
I had myself been struck by the almost unheard note of sadness: *aieí* . . .
For centuries the pedestal had been built into the wall of a church
where the worshippers' clothing
had brushed against the stone
shining it so that it glowed all the time.
There were signs of damage:
someone had tried to erase these pagan words . . .
The church lies twenty-five kilometers south of Marathon
not far from the field
on which the stone statue was dug up
on May 18, 1972.

Archaic was the smile of that morning.
The farmer recovered his field.
Lightly Phrasikleia put her foot on the pedestal.

VI

PROPERTIUS MISTRANSLATED

At first I was totally convinced it wasn't her.
Coolly telling myself as much,
I dismissed the very notion from my mind
as if I wanted nothing so much as to forget about it.
But now I could see clearly that it was Cynthia and no one else
who was sitting there on the driver's right
in the shiny red Ferrari.
Her sunglasses made her seem deliberately anonymous.
And it was certainly not in the traffic jam at the Piazza Venezia
that I expected to see her.
I search for a while in my memory—
was it a year toward the end of the sixties?
Maybe the last of April?
The driver's wearing glistening sunglasses too.
I imagine this must be the "Propertius expert"
whom she mentioned once
and who had now offered to take her to Lanuvium
in order to look at the landscape
near Juno Sospita's temple mentioned in one of the poems:
near the shrine, in antiquity, a way led down
to a cave under the rock
where a swelling snake had made his home . . .
The phallic symbolism makes me uneasy.
Suddenly, Cynthia's lipstick is as deep a red as the car
driven by the expert on Propertius who is
dressed in a summer suit, driving gloves, and a tie.
As for me, I don't even have a license!
He is rumored to be exceptionally promising
in his particular field, the Roman love elegy.
In my view, however, he is merely
yet another careerist pedant,
an Italian with an unreserved admiration
for the German philological method.

What on earth can Cynthia have seen in him?
Her silk scarf is streaming in the wind
as they disappear down the Via dei Fori Imperiali . . .
At this point, the Latin original dictates that
I must be overcome with jealousy
although in fact I feel nothing more than disappointment.
The translator is left to himself,
sitting there all alone with his poem!
And here I guess he might as well give up
since he is not blinded by jealousy
and also cannot summon up
the almost supernatural determination
that's required to invite two prostitutes back home
and revenge himself on Cynthia
with their help. What an enterprise!
I lose my breath at the very thought.
Yet here I am in the dimly lit room of the poem,
there are palms and draperies,
the room is untidy as after a party.
I have doubtless had more wine to drink than is good for me
while Phyllis and Teia
—those are the names given in the original—
are lying naked by me in the bed.
Phyllis gets up, walks across the floor to the gramophone,
and puts on some better background music.
Teia clings to me, turns me around,
and tells me ardently to kiss her breasts . . .
But I neither hear nor see.
In my mind's eye what I see is Cynthia
back in that Ferrari speeding on toward Lanuvium.
She gesticulates and laughs.
"The expert" sits self-satisfied at the wheel
driving very fast due south on the Via Appia Nuova.
Umbrella pines are passing by . . .
Suddenly I hear a key in the outer door.

I turn all cold—
The moment after Cynthia steps in the room
her silhouette seems immense,
behind her glares the bright light in the hall.
She is tall and furious.
First she attacks Phyllis and Teia,
tearing their hair, scratching them so they bleed,
making them flee half dressed into the night . . .
As the street gate closes
you can hear the neighbors talking excitedly.
After a while silence is restored.
Everyone on the block can go back to sleep.
Then in the flat the two of us are left alone—
Propertius's Swedish translator and the young woman
who was to reign supreme in the elegy.
We are standing eye to eye in the night.
She smacks my face, once, twice . . . As a Swede,
I find it difficult to understand her jealousy,
theatrical, infantile in the Latin manner . . . By what right
does she make these claims on me?
It is not I who was unfaithful . . .
Oh no! She never was unfaithful, she assures me,
pointing to a line in a poem
there in the book on my desk.
I take her word for it.
"Traduttore, traditore," she adds. As if I . . .
Disarmed, I accept my punishment:
to make the bed with new sheets in the elegy.
She is beautiful. Pale. Her lipstick is gone.
At long last we make peace.

SNOWFALL IN THE ROMAN WORLD EMPIRE

On this particular winter afternoon in the Roman World Empire
two figures are standing at the edge of the forest:
right now it is snowing so heavily
that at any distance the reader
can't make out who these two might be,
but I who am writing the poem
know that the man to the left is Göran Printz-Påhlson
wearing an immense sheepskin coat
of a Boeotian make,
and that his interlocutor is Nemesianus,
the ancient author of a number of bucolic poems
but above all of a poem on the chase,
Cynegetica, whose very beginning
is so exhortatory that many should have found it worthy of imitation.
What the two poets are discussing
is not hunting in the literal sense
but the hunt as a poetic figure, the snaring of the motif
in an ingeniously applied hunting net,
dogs barking and horns blaring . . . .
Horns blaring!—At this very moment I am fully awake.
We are standing in the FNAC in Paris,
it is the day before Christmas Eve 1978,
there is enormous congestion in the rue de Rennes just outside,
and even in the shop you can hear the honking of the cars.
Carrying a heavy load of books,
Göran tries with little success to reach the checkout desk.
It is snowing heavily. The shop is incredibly crowded.
As for myself, I am buying the Budé edition of Hesiod,
which I should have acquired a long time ago.
Göran's cheeks are unusually red.
Big flakes of snow have alighted on his beard
and are now starting to melt.
"Father Christmas, I presume?"

a voice asks in the crowd.
The question seems apposite today
though he is not wearing a pixie cap
but a Boeotian felt hat to protect himself against the northern wind—
and of course the aforementioned coat, sewn from lambskins
in the manner prescribed by Hesiod.
For the northern wind is keen, pierces
cowskins and goatskins, can only be stopped
by lambskin with wool of the thickest kind.
It makes the woods of the cosmos "bellow,"
in the phrase of the Boeotian bard,
who then proceeds to make the most of the storm,
conjuring up to great advantage in his poem
the attractions of the Boeotian farm cottage's intimate sphere.
By the light of the fire a shimmering girl
is rising anadyomenically out of her bath.
Hesiod would probably have liked to go into great detail here.
But there he is out in the snowfall!
The visibility is so poor that not even the slopes of Helicon can be seen.
We might have wanted to knock at the door ourselves
and look into the cottage
—had we only been able to get that far.
The crowd is compact.
Göran seems gigantic in his lambskin coat.
In the very moment when he hands over his Boeotian credit card
to the curiously familiar girl at the checkout desk
—doesn't she seem to have just risen out of her bath?—
we are transported to a snowed-up corner
of the northern part of the Roman World Empire.
Did the Romans get as far as Göinge?
It has stopped snowing.
Göran mutters something about "the fence
by which realism is a neighbor of Romanticism"
and at the same moment I see the stakes emerging from the snow—
some little distance from the forest

where we first discovered him.
Somehow we got on through the checkout line.
Nemesianus disappeared without a trace;
the bus for Hässleholm had already left by three o'clock.
I ask Göran what happened to the books that he bought
but for some reason he doesn't answer.
He is silent as the eagle-owl
when the stars come on.

THE STARLINGS

Late one afternoon in October
I hear them for the first time:
loud-voiced palavering, whistles, murmurs,
quarrels, bickering and warbling, croaking and chatter
in the high plane trees of the street.
The leaves are all turning yellow this time of year,
causing huge yellow sunlit rooms
to appear at the level of the fifth and sixth floors
opposite the barracks, where the tram turns off
from the Via delle Milizie.
Solid branches, twigs, and perches:
every bit of space is taken up in this parliament of starlings!
They are tightly bunched together there among the leaves;
and the hundreds of thousands of starlings
that perform their flying exercises
against the backdrop of the evening's mass of motionless cloud
will surely soon have lost their places:
there are myriads of swarming punctuation marks out there,
starlings flying in formation,
sudden sharp turns, steep ascents,
swarm on delightful swarm
against a rosy cloud bank in the east.
The October evening is cool.
The shop windows of the Via Ottaviano are shining.
And the starlings are chattering, quarreling and laughing,
whispering and quietly enjoying themselves, when suddenly
a blustering as of ten thousand pairs of sharp-edged scissors
passes through the republic of the plains—
it is as though an alarm had sounded,
heard as an echo over the muffled traffic.
Soon the darkness of night will fall.
But the starlings up there won't stop talking,
they move together, push one another, chatter and flit.

Virgil must have had them in mind when somewhere he likens
the souls of the deceased to flights of birds
which toward sundown
abandon the mountains and gather in high trees.
I seem to be standing in an Underworld
in the midst of a swarm of birds.
The block is Virgilian; the street is crossed
by the Viale Giulio Cesare,
where you lived
for some time before you died.
That's why I am stopping here.
The souls of the dead have gathered in the trees.
Their number is incredible, suddenly it seems ghastly:
is this what it will be like?
For a moment I am a prisoner
of the poem I am writing.
There must be an exit.
The soldier coming up to me
has noticed that I have been standing
for quite some time looking up into the foliage—
into the darkness of feathers, bird's eyes, and beaks.
The peasant boy inside him apprises me
of the fact that starlings come in vast migrations
"from Poland and Russia"
to spend the winter in the south:
"They certainly know how to look after themselves!
In the daytime they fly out to the countryside
and spend the night in here,"
he explains with great amusement, turning his gaze
up toward the swarm of birds. Their anxiety seems to have ceased;
in just a moment they all seem to have fallen asleep.
Only single chirps and clucks are heard
from starlings talking in their sleep.
What are they dreaming of? Ten thousand starlings are dreaming in the
    darkness

about the sunlight over the fields.
As for myself, I am thinking of the tranquility
in certain restaurants in the countryside,
in the Albano Mountains and on the Campagna—
the tranquility at noon on a sunny day in October.
I am filled with the clarity of the fall day.
And am touched by something immeasurable, transparent,
which I cannot describe at first
but must be everything we never said to each other.
There are so many things I'd like to say.
How shall I be able to speak?
Today you are not shade, you are light.
And in the poem I am writing you will be my guest.
We are going to talk about Digenís Akrítas,
the Byzantine heroic poem
with the strangely compelling rhythm;
and since the manuscript of the poem
is preserved in the monastery at Grottaferrata
I shall order wine from Grottaferrata,
golden and shimmering in its carafe;
we shall talk about the miraculously translucent autumn poem by Petronius
which appears first in Ekelöf's *Elective Affinities;*
and about Ekelöf's poems, to which you devoted such attention.
Did Ekelöf ever come to Grottaferrata?
I seem to detect your lively gaze.
And we shall see how the starlings come flying
across the fields in teeming swarms.
They will come from Rome and spend the day out here
where they will eat snails, worms, and seeds
and suddenly they will fly up from a field
as at a given signal
and make us look into the sun.

—IN MEMORIAM LUDOVICA KOCH (1941–93)

POSTSCRIPT
Lars-Håkan Svensson

"The Starlings," the last and most recent poem of this selection of Jesper Svenbro's poetry, begins with the speaker watching a swarm of starlings incessantly flitting to and fro in their "sunlit rooms" somewhere in central Rome on a sunny October afternoon. It is a compelling image of noisy, unruly vitality. However, as evening falls and the starlings settle down to sleep in the branches of the trees, the speaker is reminded of a famous passage in Virgil's *Aeneid* that compares the souls of the dead to birds. The change of mood linked to this association momentarily results in writer's block ("For a moment I am a prisoner / of the poem I am writing"), dispelled by the sudden appearance of a soldier who—acting as the speaker's guide in his private Roman underworld—comments reassuringly on the starlings: "They certainly know how to look after themselves!" In the poem's final section, the speaker imagines that the birds are transported in their dreams to a beautiful October afternoon on the Roman Campagna. This peaceful, transparent, sun-drenched vision conjures up another presence, so far only subtly hinted at: that of a deceased friend, the Italian scholar and translator Ludovica Koch, who was a connoisseur of Swedish poetry, in particular of the work of Gunnar Ekelöf, who, in his turn, wrote magnificent poems about Italy and Rome. The poem's complicated chain of private and literary associations gives way in the final lines to a literally dazzling sight: flying up from a field, the starlings cause the two friends to "look into the sun."

"The Starlings" contains several features characteristic of Svenbro's mature manner. To begin with, the format of the poem is that of a casual, seemingly autobiographical monologue, a rambling, anecdotal, diarylike narrative. The initial impression of simplicity is deceptive, however. Not only is the text shot through with striking metaphors and dense allusions; on closer inspection, the quotidian situation or memory that has caught the narrator's fancy more often than not turns out to develop into a rich symbolical or structural pattern, though these features are never insisted on, but merely intimated. The speaker remains largely the same from poem to poem; acutely aware of his origins in northern Europe, he is also closely familiar with the culture and everyday life of continental and Mediterranean Europe. His keen interest in etymology, myth, allusion, and metapoetic commentary suggests that like Svenbro he is a scholar, well versed in the linguistic and discursive ruses of contemporary academia. This is especially noticeable in poems of the 1970s and 1980s; in later works, the speaker's considerable learning is usually implied, not displayed.

Though not exploited in "The Starlings," the first and probably most important *donnée* of Svenbro's poetic universe is his provincial southern Swedish background. Born in 1944 in the small coastal town of Landskrona (with the island of Hven, where Tycho Brahe resided, and Copenhagen within sight on the horizon), he spent the first two decades of his life in this small, homogeneous community which was in many ways typical of the (then) ongoing success story of the Swedish welfare state. His personal circumstances were marked by a devastating early loss, though: in 1952 his father, a well-known and respected Landskrona clergyman, drowned. At school, he took five languages, including Latin and Greek, but also immersed himself in poetry, with T. S. Eliot (then of course at the height of his fame), Rimbaud, assorted French and Spanish modernists, and contemporary Swedish poets such as Gunnar Ekelöf, Lasse Söderberg, and Tomas Tranströmer as his masters. In 1964 Svenbro began to study Latin and Greek at Lund University. In 1969 to 1970 he spent a year at Yale, where he studied Greek with Eric Havelock, got involved in student politics, and met his future wife. In 1976 he presented his doctoral thesis at Lund (*La Parole et le marbre*). By then he had already moved abroad, first to Rome and later to Paris, where he has resided since the early 1980s when he took up a position at the CNRS (Centre National de la Recherche Scientifique). Apart from numerous journal articles, he has published two major scholarly works on Greek culture, both of them originally written in French but available in English translation: *Phrasikleia: An Anthropology of Reading in Ancient Greece* (Cornell University Press, 1993) and *The Craft of Zeus: Myths of Weaving and Fabric* (with John Scheid; Harvard University Press, 1996). As the titles indicate, his scholarly work centers on the interaction of language, myth, and social customs in ancient Greece. A collection of essays on related topics, *Myrstigar: Figurer för skrift och läsning i antikens Grekland* (*Ant-Paths: Figures of Writing and Reading in Ancient Greece*), was published to great acclaim in Sweden in 1999 and was followed in 2002 by *Fjärilslära: Antika, barocka och samtida figurer för det skrivna ordet och läsandet* (*Lepidopterology: Ancient, Baroque, and Contemporary Figures of Writing and Reading*).

Svenbro's first volume of poetry, *Det är i dag det sker* (*It Happens Today*), appeared in 1966. Its unusual mixture of youthful exuberance and witty classicism attracted some notice; in particular, critics were baffled by the concluding imitation of Virgil's *Georgics*, whose didacticism was modernized to fit contemporary Swedish agriculture and rendered in impeccable verse (one of its most memorable feats being the incorporation of the brand name of Bolínder-Munktéll, makers of tractors, into a perfect line of accentual hexameter). Incidentally, this was the first indication that Svenbro is, among other things, an accomplished formal poet, with virtuoso translations of Sappho, Rilke, and Mallarmé to his credit.

In the late 1960s and 1970s strong political pressures were brought to bear on Swedish poets, and the kind of poetry Svenbro's first collection represented was questioned on ideological grounds. This new climate seriously affected the leading poets of the day, in some cases with deplorable results. Svenbro was by no means insensitive to the changes (some of the essays he wrote during this period indicate that he was sympathetic with them politically, if not artistically) and did not write much for a long time. When he eventually brought out a new collection after a thirteen-year interval, *Element till en kosmologi* (*Elements for a Cosmology*, 1979), his new outlook was reflected both in his treatment of form and in his choice of subject matter. He now wrote poetry that, for all its studied austerity, spoke loud and clear about its precarious status as a linguistic artifact. The act of writing poetry is constantly alluded to in these poems, if it is not their explicit subject matter. For the triumphant hexameter of his first volume he substitutes a rigorous metrical pattern he had come across in the work of the Spanish poet Jorge Guillén and rhymes ordinary words of Germanic origin with sophisticated loanwords from French, Latin, or Greek. In Swedish, the effects of such rhyming are deliciously bewildering; regrettably, for obvious linguistic reasons, it has been impossible to include any of these remarkable poems here.

The metapoetic stance adopted in these and other early poems was developed under the influence of various important models. The first of these is Francis Ponge, a selection of whose prose poems Svenbro translated into Swedish in 1977. According to Ponge, the material form of a poem should correspond to its subject matter: "to each poem its poetics." This notion is important to Svenbro, as appears from an article originally published in 1980 in which he coined the term "mimopoeia" in conscious emulation of Pound's classical terms "logopoeia," "phanopoeia," and "melopoeia." The poet's job is not to conceal the act of creation but to highlight it. If this sounds arid, it should immediately be pointed out that, like Ponge, Svenbro has a keen sense of humor, and mimopoeia's humorous dimension is very important to him. By making us laugh, mimopoeia simultaneously threatens linguistic "transparency" and "the dictatorship of concepts over object," thus serving as an antiauthoritarian and subversive force.

Some of these ideas are closely related to the poetic theories and practice of the Swedish poet Göran Printz-Påhlson. Svenbro had discovered Ponge partly through an extremely influential critical study of modern Swedish poetry published in 1958 by Printz-Påhlson, another Lund man, who taught Scandinavian literature for many years at Cambridge University. An outstanding poet as well as a critic, Printz-Påhlson fueled Svenbro's mimopoetic imagination in both capacities. Significantly, Svenbro further developed his theory of mimopoeia in another essay devoted to one of Printz-Påhlson's poems, in which Svenbro sees Harry Houdini escaping from a water tank as a type of the poet.

A third important experience in this connection was Svenbro's discovery of contemporary Italian poetry, which after a decade of restraint underwent a remarkable metamorphosis in the 1970s: suddenly it was possible to write "orphic poetry, political poetry, narrative and gestural verse," as Svenbro wrote in an article in 1980. When he moved to Italy, happy circumstances soon put him in touch with several of the leading figures of this generation, in particular the Roman poet Valentino Zeichen. Zeichen alerted him to various ways in which linguistic material of a supposedly nonliterary kind could be incorporated in poetry—as metaphor, as stylistic resonance, or simply as it is.

It is easy to see how Svenbro capitalized on these ideas. In his third and fourth collections, *Särimner* (1984) and *Hermes kofösaren* (*Hermes the Cowboy*, 1991), he deliberately made use of "unpoetic" topics and adopted a self-ironic expository style closely related to dull academic or bureaucratic prose. No subject seemed forbidden to him: the making of cheese, hydropower, French ladies' underwear, the gold standard. Though dazzling the reader by the sheer force of their intellectual and artistic ingenuity, these poems also, despite their prosaic, pseudoacademic tone, at times tease the reader in a more serious way by seeming to talk about something deeply personal, a shared memory or experience that is, however, never explicitly identified or referred to as such.

The impersonal, if intellectually impeccable, manner of these early poems with their submerged autobiographical content appears not to have satisfied Svenbro in the long run. A careful reader of his third, fourth, and fifth collections could discern how each volume seems to lead up to a new position, sound a more personal tone that was then taken for granted and continued in the next collection. An English-speaking audience might have noticed a similar development in Seamus Heaney's early collections. Slowly (so slowly, in fact, that very few critics noticed it at the time), Svenbro began to broach subject matter of a more openly autobiographical nature while superficially remaining true to his earlier mode. In his later collections, *Samisk Apollon* (*Samian Apollo*, 1993), *Blått* (*Blue,* 1993), *Vid budet att Santo Bambino di Aracoeli slutligen stulits av maffian* (*On Learning That the Santo Bambino di Aracoeli Has Finally Been Stolen by the Mafia,* 1996), and *Installation med miniatyrflagga* (*Installation with a Miniature Flag,* 1999), the previously restrained or concealed autobiographical impulse emerges as the dominant force, relegating the metapoetic or mimopoetic components to a less noticeable place (though never entirely banishing them). In these poems from his full maturity, Svenbro frequently revisits his childhood and youth in Landskrona with occasional glimpses of his travels in Europe and his sojourn in the United States. He savors his anecdotal materials but also sensitively examines and queries himself and others. Not having alluded to the loss of his father in his earlier works, he now, in a series of moving poems, imagines his parents' courtship and, in his most recent book to date (*Pastorn min far* [*My Father the Vicar*], 2001), addresses the memory of his upbringing and his drowned father, devoting an entire volume to a poetic meditation on notes his father made for a study group on Revelations as a possible (and impossible) analog of World War II.

Basically, the present selection of Svenbro's poetry is arranged in chronological order, though we have also adopted a loose thematic pattern that in some cases results in the chronological order being disrupted slightly. Regrettably, neither Svenbro's very early work nor his most recent book is included, as they pose difficulties that the translators have not felt able to master. For similar reasons we have felt constrained to omit a number of poems from Svenbro's middle collections, either because they are too imbued in Swedish conditions to make much sense in English translation or because they depend on puns or linguistic effects that are untranslatable.

Translating these poems has been a very unusual and rewarding experience. Having met Jesper Svenbro in 1955 (when we both entered the same class in Landskrona) and remained in close touch with him ever since, I have had the privilege first of experiencing in his company not a few of the events that triggered the poems in this book, then reading the poems in Swedish, often while they were still fresh from the mint, and finally reliving and reimagining them while translating them into English. This last enterprise would not have been possible had it not been for John Matthias, who suggested that we translate Svenbro's poems in the first place and later proved a selfless, resourceful, and indefatigable collaborator; I am convinced that he must by now stand very well with Stiernhielm's *Musae Suethizantes*. Although I have had the pleasure of visiting John a number of times in Indiana, most of the actual work has been done by e-mail. The hazards and joys of electronic translation are best conveyed by the following poem by John Matthias, which is included at Jesper Svenbro's suggestion:

The Cotranslator's Dilemma

Again the e-mail draft appears on my screen.
I go back to work.
Tranströmer's successor speaks aloud from his poem.
Sort of, that is. I'm supposed to make such improvements

that everyone in America will recognize at a flash
the original style & voice, the very personality of this poet
known up to now only by his most intimate friends.
I despair. They are waiting in Lund for my version.
But it's already in English, so what should I do?
I change an article: "*The* cow in the pasture" would really
be better written here "*A* cow in the pasture."
I stare at the screen. Maybe a comma just before the conjunction.
At just that moment I hear a commotion in the hall.
I can hear several people questioning students:
Which is the charlatan's office? I recognize the Swedish accents.
Suddenly Jesper and Leif, Göran and Lars-Håkan
all tumble into my room. We're here to help you, they laugh.
Göran offers me a virtual beer.
The heart of your problem, Leif says in Swedish,
is that you don't know Swedish. What?
He says in English: the problem is that you don't know Swedish.
Oh, that. Well, I work from this other guy's drafts.
What do you do? He seems to have a whole list of questions.
I show him the screen: "*A* cow" was once "*The* cow," I say,
and commas, or their absence, are very important.
That's it? he asks. Nothing else?
Well, there's the issue of prepositions. I find that most
of my Swedish colleagues get confused:
A poet whose head is up in the clouds may appear with
his head up *around* the clouds, or up *about* the clouds,
or even up *from* or up *off* the clouds!
The four Swedes sputter with amusement or contempt.
So that's all? Articles, prepositions, and commas?
Well, sometimes, if I'm lucky.
And what if you're not? Not lucky, that is.
Ah, then—I hesitate—then I have to rewrite the poem.
You'd rewrite somebody's poem?
Not in Swedish, of course, I hasten to say. Just in English.
Ah well, they grumble, that's a relief.

I mean, what can you do with a poem set entirely in Lapland
that's full of *yoiks* and *vuolles*? And then he throws in
classical myths and quotes not only from Sappho but also Rimbaud.
American readers will never sort it all out.
American readers could learn to yoik for themselves, Jesper insists.
In the poem with a cow? I mean, I say,
in the poem that appeared on my screen containing *the* cow.
The one whose poet had his head up around the clouds.
Apollo and Hermes are also, I can see, there on the screen,
and what I am to do with words like *Poikilóthronos* and *Boukólos?*
Well, Lars-Håkan says, what *will* you do?
I'll change the setting entirely, move the lot of them to Texas!
But in Texas nobody yoiks, everybody protests.
There are plenty of cows, however, and cowboys like to yell & shout
while they ride all around saying things like "Yahoo!"
But a yoik is a Lapland poem, it's a chant, an incantation, a song!
In my Texas version the cowboys will sing quite a lot:
"Git along little dogie," and stuff like that.
That's the line in fact that I'll substitute for the quote from Rimbaud.
What about Hermes? What about Apollo?
I think I'll exchange them for John Wayne & Clint Eastwood.
Those are mythic types American readers relate to.
All the Swedes have now stopped grinning & laughing
And are starting to cry, tearing their hair.
In Greek plays lots of people cry and tear their hair.
That's another thing that gets into this poem, along with the
language itself: the *Poikilóthronoses* and *Boukóloses.*
Sounds like some bacteria infecting the meat of the burger.
Göran says, darting a knowing glance over at Jesper:
the author of this poem is an eminent Hellenist!
By God, I thought he was a Swede!
Anyway, if you've got to have your Greek go see Ezra Pound.
He's long dead, of course, which means
You might as well just go on working with me.
I've become a little tipsy by this point drinking the virtual beer

and suddenly drop the nearly empty virtual bottle onto the keyboard.
Yoiks! We're all at once transported off to Amazon.com.
The Amazon: now that's better than Texas!
The stern-wheeler is sailing upriver from Santarém.
Elizabeth Bishop is getting on board, clutching
an empty wasp's nest given to her by the druggist
in the town's little blue pharmacy. I follow her with my cow
which has somehow attracted a herd—
not of cattle exactly, but of sheep, goats, yaks,
chickens, llamas, cats, and yellow dogs.
What's going on? I'm not exactly sure, but I like it.
Jesper's shouting in English: Who do you think you are,
some kind of Hercules? That poem (that golden girdle!) is mine;
I, I, I, am Tranströmer's successor!
Not anymore, I exclaim, heading into the current
on the riverboat called *Poikilóthronos Juan.*
Off in wintry Lund, all the systems start to crash.
Every screen flickers and goes blank.

TRANSLATORS' NOTES

GENERAL NOTE: Swedish place-names have been translated in a few cases in which the literal meaning of the name is important to the understanding of the poem as a whole. Some poems make use of words and expressions of Lap—or, as we now say, Saami—origin: a "yoik" (*jojk*) or "vuolle" is a chant, usually improvised, inspired by, and commemorating some important event or person in the singer's life. A "jokk" (compare Johann Sebastian Jokk in "Once-Only Music") is a rill. A "naoid" (*nåjd*) is a shaman able to interpret the will of the gods of the pre-Christian Saami religion. "Arra" is the Saami word for hearth (*"Campus Elysii"*).

Stalin as Wolf

The poem is partly based on an article titled "Les Loups au festin ou la Cité impossible" (in M. Detienne, J.-P. Vernant, and others, *La Cuisine du sacrifice en pays grec* [Paris: 1979]; *The Cuisine of Sacrifice among the Greeks* [Chicago: 1989]) and was originally written for Stalin's one-hundredth anniversary.

Lepidopterology

Georg Stiernhielm (1598–1672), a scholar, scientist, and public official, has been called the father of Swedish poetry. His main literary achievement is a long philosophical poem in hexameter, *Hercules,* while "Silkesmasken" ("The Silk-Worm") is usually thought to be the first sonnet written in Swedish. The silkworm is a motif found in seventeenth-century emblem books, where it symbolizes spiritual regeneration or love's restorative power. In a recent essay, Svenbro ventures to read Stiernhielm's sonnet as an ancient Greek might have read it ("Silkesmasken och fjärilen," *Fjärilslära* [Stockholm: 2002]).

Coastal Defense

On the night of October 27, 1981, the Soviet submarine U-137 ran aground in Gåsefjärden (Goose Bay), a prohibited military area on Sweden's southeastern coast, and finally had to accept the Swedish navy's assistance in order to be able to return to international waters. *Sänka skepp* (here literally rendered as "sink-a-ship") is a schoolchildren's game played on square-ruled paper.

Kit for an Orpheus Poem

The Swedish words *lyra* (lyre) and *ljud* (sound) carry the additional meaning "wound on a tree," as appears from, for example, *Lexicon forestale* (Porvoo, Finland: 1979). The passage about Orpheus and the Argonauts contains an allusion to Olof Rudbeck's *Atlantica* (1679–1702). Rudbeck (1630–1702) was a prodigiously learned scholar and professor of medicine at Uppsala University who willfully, implausibly, and ingeniously set out to prove that after the Deluge Scandinavia had been sought out by Japhet, whose descendants had later settled in Greece. Consequently, Greek had developed out of Swedish and Greek myths out of Scandinavian mythology; in *Atlantica* (1.xxvi), Rudbeck contends that the "Pontus Axenis" (the Euxine) is in fact identical to "dhen Euxiniske Botn" on account of the similarity between "Botn"—the present-day Bothnia—(Swedish *botten*, English "bottom") and "Pontus" (Greek for "sea").

Mont Blanc
The "young English wanderer" is of course William Wordsworth, who in his *Descriptive Sketches* (written in 1791 and 1792) provides an account of his walks near Mont Blanc.

Cynegetics
In Severin Solders' Greek grammar, used in Swedish schools, *thēreúō* (I hunt) is the verb exemplifying the first conjugation. Cynegetics (the art of hunting) is derived from *kúōn* (dog) and *hēgeîsthai* (to lead).

The Vuolle of Mount Ammar
Mount Ammar is situated in the southern part of (Swedish) Lapland.

Sweden's Helicon
Applying the Rudbeckian method of etymological analogy (see note on "Kit for an Orpheus Poem"), Svenbro here humorously treats "Vindelfjäll" as a Swedish equivalent of "Helicon": Swedish *vindel* and Greek *hélix* both mean "spiral"; the names of the two mountains would thus both mean "Mount Spiral." The three lines spoken by the Nine Clouds travesty a passage at the beginning of Hesiod's *Theogony* (lines 26–28). Before tradition codified the name of Orpheus's paramour she was called Agriope, which means "wild voice." The title contains an allusion to a famous Elizabethan anthology of (mainly) pastoral verse: *Englands Helicon* (1600).

Campus Elysii
Oulavuolie (Ulevuole, "Mount Ol") is known from "The Reindeer on Oula-

vuolie," a magnificent yoik by Nils Mattias Andersson. The poem's title alludes to Olof Rudbeck's botanical volume of prints of the same name (Stockholm: 1701–2).

Poikilóthronos Sappho
Cape Dårra (Dårraudden) is situated near Lake Stora Tjulträsk in southern Lapland. During a period a nomad school was kept there in three Saami huts of a traditional shape (*kåta*). *Poikilóthronos* is the first word of the ode that used to introduce Sappho's collected works; this particular ode is now the only poem by Sappho preserved in its entirety. Svenbro wrote an article on the meaning of the word in which he argues that *poikilóthronos* means "adorned with variegated flowers" rather than "seated on a richly worked throne" (see *Le Métier de Zeus: Mythe du tissage et du tissu dans le monde gréco-romain* [Paris: 1994], 61–70; *The Craft of Zeus: Myths of Weaving and Fabric* [Cambridge, Mass.: 1996], 53–82).

The Fountain of Dark Mountain
This poem again, in Rudbeck fashion, plays on the similarity between Mörkfjäll (Dark Mountain) and Skotoessa (the dark one), the name of a town in Thessaly. For Skotoessa, see Aristotle, *On Marvellous Things Heard*, 117.

Three-Toed Gull, Sighted Near the Lighthouse of Kullen
The Sound referred to here—and occasionally elsewhere—is the sound, also known as Öresund, between Denmark and Sweden. A southerner like Svenbro, the composer Lars-Erik Larsson (1908–86), perhaps best known for his neo-Romantic *Pastoral Suite* (1938), was born near Lund and retired in 1971 to the coastal town of Helsingborg.

Cowpath
Martin P. Nilsson (1874–1967) is one of Lund University's most famous twentieth-century scholars and the author of internationally renowned works on Greek religion and religiosity.

At the Grave of C. F. Hill
Carl Fredrik Hill (1849–1911), the son of a Lund professor of mathematics, painted a series of magnificent landscapes in France in the 1870s. However, before being recognized, he suffered a mental breakdown and had to return to Lund. Cared for by his family, he would produce up to four chalk drawings a day, many of which anticipate later developments in modern art.

Tranströmer Epigones
Tuborg, also known for its brewery, is a suburb of Copenhagen that in the period referred to in the poem had a daily ferry service to Landskrona. "Weather Picture" is the title of an early Tranströmer poem.

The X
Sven Erixson (1899–1970), often referred to as the X, was a highly acclaimed painter known for his idiosyncratic fusion of realism, expressionism, and naivism.

Exploded Haiku
One of the pioneers of poetic modernism in Sweden, Erik Lindegren (1910–68) wrote an important sequence of "exploded sonnets" in 1942 entitled *Mannen utan väg* (*The Man without a Way*).

Snowfall in the Roman World Empire
Göran Printz-Påhlson (see postscript) was born in Hässleholm, a small town in a part of southern Sweden known as Göinge (see also "Cowpath").

The Starlings
Goethe of course famously wrote a novel entitled *The Elective Affinities*. The Swedish poet Gunnar Ekelöf (1907–68) appropriated the title for an influential volume of translations.

The Cotranslator's Dilemma
The fourth Swedish voice prophetically overheard by John Matthias in this poem is that of Leif Sjöberg (1925–2000). Sjöberg, for many years a professor at SUNY and Columbia, was a tutelary spirit of Swedish poetry, himself responsible for many translations of Swedish poems into English.

Jesper Svenbro was born in 1944 in the small town of Landskrona in southern Sweden. An internationally renowned classical scholar, he studied classics at Lund University and Greek with Eric Havelock at Yale, has lived in Italy, and now lives in France, where he has for many years held a post at the Centre National de la Recherche Scientifique. His poetry has been translated into French, German, and Italian, and he is the recipient of numerous awards in his native country.